P9-ECQ-187

*Canadian Biography Series*

TIMOTHY FINDLEY: STORIES FROM A LIFE

*This 1991 portrait by Alan Dayton hangs in*
*the dining room at Stone Orchard, a gift from*
*William Whitehead to Timothy Findley.*

# Timothy Findley

STORIES FROM A LIFE

## Carol Roberts

ECW PRESS

Copyright © ECW PRESS, 1994

CANADIAN CATALOGUING IN PUBLICATION DATA

Roberts, Carol
Timothy Findley : stories from a life

Includes bibliographical references.
ISBN I-55022-195-7

I. Findley, Timothy 1930–  – Biography.  2. Authors, Canadian
(English) – 20th century – Biography.*   I. Title.

PS8511.I38Z87 1994    C818 .54    C94-930591-X
PR9199.3.I38Z87 1994

This book has been published with the assistance of the Ministry
of Culture, Recreation and Tourism of the Province of Ontario,
through funds provided by the Ontario Publishing Centre, and with
the assistance of grants from the Department of Communications,
The Canada Council, the Ontario Arts Council, and the Government
of Canada through the Canadian Studies and Special Projects
Directorate of the Department of the Secretary of State of Canada.

Design and imaging by ECW Type & Art, Oakville, Ontario.
Printed by Imprimerie Gagné, Louiseville, Québec.

Distributed by General Distribution Services,
30 Lesmill Road, Toronto, Ontario M3B 2T6,
(416) 445-3333, (800) 387-0172 (Canada), FAX (416) 445-5967.

Distributed to the trade in the United States exclusively
by InBook, 140 Commerce Street, P.O. Box 120261,
East Haven, Connecticut, U.S.A. 06512,
(203) 467-4257,  FAX (203) 469-8364.
Customer service: (800) 243-0138, FAX (800) 334-3892.

Published by ECW PRESS,
1980 Queen Street East,
Toronto, Ontario M4L IJ2.

## ACKNOWLEDGEMENTS

Writing a book is nearly always a cooperative effort. For this book, I want to thank William Hutt and John Pearce who graciously shared their stories about working with Timothy Findley; Martha Henry for her written memories of him; Alan Dayton for use of his evocative portrait as the frontispiece illustration for this book; and my family, friends, and colleagues who clipped "Findley things," called to say he was on CBC Radio *right now*, proofread, explored the old Massey-Harris plant, and always listened with patience, if not fascination. My greatest debt is to Timothy Findley and William Whitehead, who have become a familiar Tiff and Bill. They have been more than generous with their time and interest, answering my many questions, sharing stories from their lives, and allowing me to choose photographs from their collection, read manuscript copies of new work, and spend two delightful days with them at Stone Orchard. Their trust, generosity, and kindness have made this project a memorable experience.

Thanks also to the Canadian Broadcasting Corporation, Elisabeth Feryn, Robert Lansdale, Brian McConnell, Robert C. Ragsdale, and Judy White for allowing me to use photographs; to Leonard Belsher of the Grand Theatre and Lisa Brant of the Stratford Festival Archives for help with photo permissions; to the National Film Board of Canada for permission to quote from *Timothy Findley: Anatomy of a Writer*; to CBC Radio's *Ideas* program for permission to quote from "Blue Is the Colour of Hope"; and to HarperCollins Publishers for permission to quote from *Inside Memory: Pages from a Writer's Workbook*.

PHOTOGRAPHS: Cover photo, 1984, Elisabeth Feryn, is used by permission of the photographer; frontispiece illustration, 1991, is used by permission of the artist, Alan Dayton; illustration 2, 1937, photographer unknown, is provided courtesy of Timothy Findley; illustration 3, 1944, photographer unknown, in provided courtesy of Timothy Findley; illustration 4, 1948, George Gibson, is provided courtesy of Timothy Findley; illustration 5, 1950, photographer unknown, is provided courtesy of Timothy Findley; illustration 6, 1953, Peter Smith, is provided courtesy of the Stratford

AUGUSTANA UNIVERSITY COLLEGE
LIBRARY

Festival; illustration 7, 1955, photographer unknown, is provided courtesy of Timothy Findley; illustration 8, 1960, and 11, 1967, Jonathan White, are used by permission of Judy White, wife of the photographer; illustration 9, 1959, is used by permission of the Canadian Broadcasting Corporation; illustration 10, 1962, photographer unknown, is provided courtesy of Timothy Findley; illustration 12, © 1977, Robert Lansdale, is used by permission of the photographer; illustration 13, 1984, Elisabeth Feryn, is used by permission of the photographer; illustration 14, 1972, is used by permission of the Canadian Broadcasting Corporation; illustration 15, 1984, Elisabeth Feryn, is used by permission of the photographer; illustration 16, 1992, Brian McConnell, is used by permission of the photographer; illustration 17, 1992, is provided courtesy of Timothy Findley; illustration 18, 1993, Robert C. Ragsdale, is used by permission of the photographer and provided courtesy of the Grand Theatre, London.

Quotations from *Inside Memory: Pages from a Writer's Workbook*, by Timothy Findley. Copyright © 1990 by Pebble Productions, Inc. Published by HarperCollins Publishers, Ltd. All rights reserved. Used by permission.

Quotations from "Blue Is the Colour of Hope." Produced by Marilyn Powell for cbc Radio's *Ideas*, 15–16 June 1992. All rights reserved. Used by permission.

Quotations from *Timothy Findley: Anatomy of a Writer*, videocassette. Dir. Terence Macartney-Filgate. National Film Board of Canada, 1992. Used by permission.

# TABLE OF CONTENTS

# LIST OF ILLUSTRATIONS

# Timothy Findley

## STORIES FROM A LIFE

Biographers, like writers of fiction, tell stories. Fiction writers work from the imagination, biographers from the life of their subject. But the "facts" of a person's life can be told as a story, or a series of stories, that resembles imaginative fiction. Stories play an important role in our lives. We experience an event, but that event acquires meaning, becomes part of our life story, only when we tell it to someone or write it down. The telling, and retelling, fixes these stories in memory.

It is fitting to write Timothy Findley's biography in this manner — using Findley's own stories and the stories of those who have known him — because Findley is himself a master storyteller. He tells stories in his fiction, yes, but he also tells stories about his life. Colleagues, interviewers, friends, students, and anyone who has attended his readings remember his tales. His actor's voice and fine sense of drama enhance the storyteller's role. The audience settles comfortably to listen, to hear his story.

### THE ROSEDALE FINDLEYS

This story begins in the exclusive Rosedale area of Toronto. In the middle of the last century, the area north of Bloor and east of Yonge Street was a pleasant parkland of wooded hills and deep ravines. The wild roses that bloomed in profusion every spring inspired Mary Jarvis, wife of the local sheriff, to name their house "Rosedale." The Jarvis estate is now South Rosedale. In 1909 a bridge was built over the Park Drive ravine to open up more land in North Rosedale for the influx of the moneyed upper classes who were leaving the urban centre for what was then open country on the edge of the fast-growing town of Toronto. The Findleys were part of this exodus to the suburbs. Many of Rosedale's original families are gone now, some to more modern houses beyond the increasingly congested city centre and some because their fortunes declined. Declining fortunes were a constant threat to the Findleys.

Today the neighbourhood retains the look of British upper-class respectability that it had when Timothy Irving Frederick Findley was born on 30 October 1930 in a spacious house on Glenrose Avenue. The Findleys lived in this house for the first two years of young Timothy's life. He has only one memory of the Glenrose house: he was afraid of the wolves that lived under the back porch steps.

The Glenrose house, with its imaginary wolves, is no longer there. In 1950 when Mount Pleasant Road was extended south to Jarvis Street, in order to route the increasing traffic off the quiet Rosedale streets, several of the neighbourhood's stately homes were razed. But at the time Findley was born, Glenrose Avenue was home to some of Toronto's best families. Frederick Banting, the discoverer of insulin, lived down the street; his son was a playmate of the young Findley boys.

Thomas Findley, Timothy's grandfather, came from rural central Ontario, not far from where his grandson now lives. Thomas's mother died in childbirth, his father shortly after from pneumonia that developed after he walked several miles in the cold rain to fetch the doctor for his dying wife. Thomas was raised by an aunt, though when he left school after grade eight, he was taken on by the Sutton Village general-storekeeper. In those days the general store also served as the area's communication centre. Young Thomas delivered the mail to the surrounding farms on horseback and subsequently learned how to use the telegraph, a skill that served him well when he left Sutton to seek his fortune. Merrill Denison, in his book on the history of the

Massey-Harris Company, writes that the story of young Thomas Findley's arrival in Toronto became something of a legend:

> Back in 1890, when the private telegraph office was still a feature of large industrial plants, Chester Massey entered the Head Office building one afternoon to find a country boy waiting in the hallway, completely immersed in a book that he was reading. No clue to its title has survived, but legend maintains it was the Bible, so favorable was the impression it made on the older man. Questioning disclosed that the lad had come in answer to an advertisement for a telegraph operator, and further questioning that he had learned the art while working in a general store in Sutton village, some thirty miles north of Toronto, not far from the farm where he was born. A letter from the store-keeper praised the boy as neat, courteous, trustworthy and diligent, and noted that he was a great reader, although he had been able to attend school for only a few years. Chester Massey liked his modest bearing and quiet air of assurance, and Tom Findley entered the employment of the Massey Manufacturing Company as a telegraph operator at $6.00 a week.

From this humble beginning, Thomas Findley rose to become president of Massey-Harris in 1917, at that time the largest farm-machinery manufacturer in the British Empire. While president, he introduced progressive labour policies: modern shop practices, a shorter workweek, rest and smoking rooms, a cafeteria, trained nurses, and first-aid facilities. Thomas Findley was admired by all who knew him. As a child, Timothy Findley remembers that he was lauded as a great man, so great that his sons and grandsons were told they could never even aspire to be like him.

The Thomas Findleys were a respected Rosedale family, active in the Presbyterian church and society life. The *Torontonian Society Blue Book and Club List* for 1919 records the many service and social clubs to which Thomas, his wife Phoebe, and the three children belonged. However, the good times were destined to end abruptly. Thomas Findley died of cancer in 1921, leaving his wife, a daughter, Margaret, and two sons with serious financial troubles and a sense of having come down in the world.

The elder son, Thomas Irving Findley, served in France during World War I and was seriously wounded when his plane was shot down; he died of his injuries many years later. Visits to Uncle Tif, Timothy Findley's godfather, are one of Findley's earliest memories and constitute an often-told story. He writes in his memoir, *Inside Memory*:

> Uncle Tif — who died at home — was always in a great tall bed — high up — and the bed was white. I would go into his room, supported by my father's hands, and lean against the lower edge of the mattress. There was a white sheet over everything, and I can smell that sheet to this day. It smelled of soap and talcum powder. To me, Uncle Tif was a hand that came down from a great way off and tapped me on the head. . . . And high above my head, there was a tall glass jar on a table and the jar was full of hard French candies. They had shiny jackets and were many colours. And Uncle Tif's hand would go out, waving in the air above my gaze and lift up the lid of the jar and take out a candy and slowly — it was always slowly — he would pass the candy down into my open mouth.

Allan — the younger son and Findley's father — became a stockbroker and aspired to restore the family's fortune and social position. Findley's parents met on a piano bench, a fitting introduction since Margaret Bull's father owned a piano factory in the same area of rural Ontario where Allan's father grew up. As Findley tells the story, Margaret sat down beside her future husband as he played the piano at a party and never left his side.

Findley adored his maternal grandmother, Edith Maude Bull, who stayed with the family for extended periods of time. Findley described this first storyteller in his life to Elspeth Cameron:

"She had total recall. In a voice that had the Irish *tone* she would recall every nuance of dress, place, and atmosphere. The incidents she spoke of were always connected to the deep past, to saints, princes, royalty. This implied a lineage. . . . It meant the king is there *in you* to be evolved. I remember her in her shawl, her hair Edwardian, singing 'The Last Rose of Summer' at the piano in a quavering wonderful voice. It was dark, sad, overlaid with 'Oh, God! The troubles, the troubles.' "

## CHILDHOOD

The Findleys did indeed have their troubles. The Depression, which followed the 1929 stock market crash, eroded Allan Findley's financial capital and the family was forced to sell their Rosedale house and move to a rented one in a less expensive area. They had to sell much of their fine furniture and the nanny and cook were replaced with a general maid. But Margaret Findley kept up appearances, dressing the boys in stylish secondhand clothes from the Junior League Shop.

In 1937 the family was able to move back to Rosedale, to a rented house on Crescent Road. There Tiff, as he was called after his Uncle Tif and his own initials, played with his pet rabbits in the garden behind the house. Over the high wall, a winding path led down through the trees to one of the several park-like ravines in the area. It was an idyllic setting for childhood, but not an idyllic childhood.

There was death and sickness in young Findley's life, followed by a wrenching separation. When Tiff was three, his infant brother died and Tiff developed double mastoids, then pneumonia. At the hospital he was given up as a terminal case, but when the doctor broke the news to Findley's parents, his mother, who had just lost one son in the same ward where Tiff was housed, refused to give up hope. Findley recalled the family story for Philip Marchand:

FIGURE 2

*A family snapshot of seven-year-old Tiff Findley.*

"My mother said, 'I'll be damned if he will die in this bloody place. I'm taking him home.' And the doctor said, 'Well, you might as well let him die at home.' And she took me home and she put me on the back porch in a baby carriage. Going home from the hospital saved me." ("Novelist on a High Wire")

A short time later, Uncle Tif died.

As a child, Tiff — who had inherited his mother's light blue eyes and blond hair — was considered delicate and was therefore protected from rough play and strenuous games. He was often sick, in hospital again at seven with appendicitis and whooping cough, missing months of school at a time. Much of his childhood he spent alone, reading *The Wind in the Willows*, *Black Beauty*, Ernest Thompson Seton and Beatrix Potter stories, playing with his pets or sitting in the kitchen with the maid for company, waiting for his mother to come through the door from wherever her life had taken her — which to young Tiff always seemed to be away from him.

The strong, compassionate maid figure appears in several of Findley's stories and novels. In "Lemonade," Findley describes one such character in his account of young Harper Dewey's breakfast and the ritual that started each day:

Bertha Millroy was the maid — and a day, to Bertha, wasn't a day at all unless it began with a hymn and ended with a prayer.

She lived — Bertha — in the attic, in a small room directly above Harper's room and she sang her hymn from the window which opened over his head. When it was finished she would say the same thing every morning — "Amen" and "Good morning, Harper." Then they would race each other to the landing on the stairs.

In contrast to Tiff, who was of a solitary nature, his older brother, Michael, was popular, robust, and skilled at games. In an early short story, "The People on the Shore," Findley gives a fictional account of their personalities:

> He was a worldly child. . . . [H]e had a great many friends and, amongst them, he was always accorded the rank of leader. In fact, he was leading now, followed by a lot of children, out towards the model shipwreck. To me — his back was his most familiar feature. I just wasn't part of the world he was trying to create: neither was he, with the exception of his back, a part of mine. My world was a place devoid of other children, pretty well. I intended it to be so: something in me — possibly perverse — didn't like other children: particularly of my own age. They seemed always to be something I was not — and to know something that was beyond my understanding.

## THE WAR

Tiff was nine when World War II erupted and Allan Findley enlisted in the air force — telling Michael before he left but saying nothing to his younger son. Tiff's terrible sense of abandonment and betrayal is vividly expressed by the young narrator in another early short story, "War":

> Maybe I just couldn't forgive him. He hadn't even told me. He didn't even write it in his letter that he'd sent me at Arthur Robertson's. But he'd told Bud — he'd told Bud, but I was the one he'd promised to show how to skate. And I'd had it all planned how I'd really surprise my dad and turn out to be a skating champion and everything, and now he wouldn't even be there to see.
>
> All because he had to go and sit in some trench.

The traumatic effect of this incident is evident from the number of times Findley tells the story in interviews and articles. He says now that it took him a very long time to forgive his father for suddenly disappearing from his life. He described to Alan Twigg how he felt when his father got his orders to go overseas:

> I'll never forget the day he learned he was going overseas. This was very late in 1943. He was home on leave. In Canada you got leave every eight weeks or so. And the thing that I always got to do was polish the buttons. When he got the phone call saying to go overseas with the next shipment of troops, he jumped up and down on the bed like a child. . . . I was seeing this grown-up doing this extraordinary thing and thinking, in whatever way a child would think, "You son-of-a-bitch. You can't wait to get away from us." I'm not sure if that was his feeling at all. . . . It was awful. Oh, it was awful!

Allan Findley's absence during the war had a more pragmatic effect as well: it increased the family's financial troubles. Margaret struggled in vain to keep up the rent payments on the house on Crescent Road, even trying her hand at writing a mystery novel to make some money, but eventually mother and sons had to leave Rosedale once again.

During the war years, Margaret was often away for months at a time, joining her husband whenever he was stationed in Canada. Tiff and Michael were sent to live with various relatives and friends, often separated, and then enrolled in St. Andrew's College, the private boarding school their father had attended. Tiff hated it with a passion. In "Christmas Remembered," a memoir written for *Chatelaine*'s 1979 Christmas issue, he wrote of the desolate winter of 1942. When Michael became seriously ill with rheumatic fever, Margaret arrived at St. Andrew's to take him away:

> But where, when we'd given up our house, could she take him to die? For we thought he was going to die and there wasn't any doubt of that. I remember vividly his leaving school in the back of a car, his face covered with blankets against the cold and my mother sitting beside him in a

brown suit and a brown hat. (Why did she have to wear brown?) I knew I would never see him again. It rained. This was November '42. The Germans were winning everything. All the Canadians — except my father — had died at Dieppe and my father was so far away it seemed impossible to think of him as real. I hadn't seen him in almost a year. We lived without a centre.

Years later Findley looked back on his child-self turning around to walk back into the hated boarding school as the car disappeared down the drive and feeling utterly abandoned. As he talked of his childhood in the 1992 National Film Board documentary, *Timothy Findley: Anatomy of a Writer*, he recalled the moment. He said he now realizes that the child in this vital memory was the incipient writer "watching with wonder the subtleties of the adult world come in and alter his life forever." The lonely and impotent child is powerless to act; he can only observe and record.

Margaret took Michael to his grandmother's house in Toronto and there Tiff joined them and his Aunt Marg, who lived with Grandmother "Goggie," for the bleak holiday. Michael recovered, but Christmas 1942 was a sad and anxious time:

We stood there, looking like refugees, standing in the middle of the floor. Huddled like the team that just lost the game. Sheep in a storm. Emigrants in a foreign country. Anything but a family. We didn't even seem to belong to one another.

Their circumstances were not improved a great deal when Allan Findley returned after the war. Findley recalled for Val Ross how, at fifteen, he experienced the situation:

"We'd lost everything. We were living in a rented house and it slowly became clear that the world was still dark. 1945, '46, '47 — I remember them as years of blizzards, bad weather, no work. My father would lie on the sofa in the dark with his hand over his head and you'd hear low moans: 'Oh, God.' It was clear he felt we'd entrapped him. He did not want us."

Sickness, death, separation — not the ingredients of a happy childhood. In an often-quoted remark to Elspeth Cameron, Findley said, "I was told, 'Childhood is the best time of your life.' Childhood was unmitigated *hell* from beginning to end. If I had been told 'Childhood has its drawbacks, hasn't it kid?' I would have been able to adjust. . . ."

## ADOLESCENCE

Adolescence was not much better. Again there were several major and minor illnesses that enlisted Margaret's unwavering efforts to protect her still-delicate son. After graduating from Rosedale Public School in 1945, Tiff attended nearby Jarvis Collegiate off-and-on where he failed to distinguish himself either scholastically or socially. A private tutor was engaged during a long bout of mononucleosis but Findley resisted his efforts, wanting only to talk about history and literature. He spent many long days in bed, recovering from illnesses — reading, daydreaming, and filling notebooks with stories of dashing heroes on horseback performing brave deeds while the doctor took endless blood tests and told him not to move.

Findley composed many long, romantic novels during those months in bed. "They were awful," Findley told me, "full of adventure and romance, kid's novels. Everybody was having great love affairs but I didn't really know what that meant. I wrote my way out of that bedroom." The manuscripts were lost in a fire years later in the house he shared briefly with his wife. An amateur photographer, she had left a chemical heating and it caught fire when they were both out of the house. Findley is sorry the stories were lost. "I would hope no one else would ever see them, but I would love to. They were great fun."

At the age of seven or eight, Findley realized he was sexually attracted to men. At fourteen he told his mother he was homosexual, and the following year he told his father, who had just returned from the war. At first their reaction was one of denial.

FIGURE 3

*The Findleys during the war: Michael, Margaret,
Allan in his air-force uniform, and Tiff, aged 14.*

In an effort to set their son on what they considered the right track, his parents saw to it that he meet many suitable girls; they " 'flung me at girls and they flung girls at me,' " as he described it to Elspeth Cameron. Both parents later accepted his homosexuality, not only with equanimity, Findley told me, but with grace.

Adolescence also marked the beginning of Findley's search for creative direction. To David MacFarlane, he spoke of " 'the perfection of gesture' " that artists seek. This quest has occupied Findley throughout his life. Dance, most closely linked to physical gesture, was his first choice of artistic medium.

## AT MASSEY-HARRIS

Faced with his father's refusal to encourage any dancing ambitions — " 'I'm damned if I'm going to pay for ballet lessons for a son of mine!' " — Tiff decided to pay for the lessons himself. At seventeen he got a job at Massey-Harris, the company in which Thomas Findley had once been president. Unlike his grandfather, Tiff wasn't discovered studiously reading in the hall; in fact, his career with the company began — and ended — in the factory's malleable department. In a *Toronto Star* series on "My First Job," he described the factory setting as "something out of Dickens":

We delivered roughly finished bits of metal to other parts of the factory. My most vivid memories were of journeys up and down in terrible, rickety elevators, which had deathly warnings all over them. Do not enter this elevator with more than so many tons of material, they would say. And I would always think, "What happens if I'm three ounces over?"

At the elevator, you opened these gigantic metal doors and you were knocked back by an absolute blast of heat. Then you opened some wooden safety doors and everything would creak and the elevator would sag about a foot as you got on. Then you'd close all the doors and pull the elevator up or down, pulling hand over hand.

When you got to the floor of the forge, you couldn't hear a thing. The noise was simply deafening.

Talking with Findley about his time working at Massey-Harris brings forth a host of stories. The seventeen-year-old Rosedale youth was simultaneously terrified and fascinated by the intense heat and noise. "It was a raging, blazing red place filled with fire," he told me. "The foundry workers were all deaf. You had to tap them on the shoulder to get their attention." Moreover, Findley was nervous about entering this raucous, masculine world, having grown up in a world almost entirely populated by women. But he was accepted as "one of the guys" and taken under the wing of a gruff but kindly old hand who remembered his grandfather.

Findley loved the early morning bus and streetcar rides through Toronto's deserted streets, the steamy coffee shop on dark winter mornings, and the feeling of belonging to a special group — those who rose with the sun to do the city's work. He recalled the society of the factory's washroom where young workers, with combs and cigarette packages protruding from back pockets, read comic books on the john and preened in front of mirrors. "The vanity in men's washrooms is simply dazzling," Findley told me, standing up and turning toward an imaginary mirror to illustrate his point. At the Massey-Harris Christmas party, he got drunk for the first time — "I took off like gang-busters after that" — then went home to the family dinner table feigning sobriety.

Many of the Massey-Harris buildings that once occupied several blocks along the lakefront in west Toronto have been torn down. A few remain and attest to the company's enormous size and activity earlier in the century. Tunnels large enough to move farm machinery under the streets, high-ceilinged workrooms, and enormous furnaces bear witness to Findley's Dickensian memories.

Handsome, broad-shouldered Tiff Findley led a double life while he worked at Massey-Harris. Hurrying home on the bus in workboots and sweaty clothes at the end of a day, he showered, changed into his dance things, and was back on the bus to ballet class. His days were spent in the company of rough workmen, his evenings with sensitive young men and women intent on an artistic life.

## FIRST ACTING ROLE

Findley's hope of finding a creative outlet in dance, however, was soon shattered. A fused disc ended his dream of dancing professionally. Findley next tried acting. As he told Elspeth Cameron:

> "I wanted to *express* something. . . . I got into an Easter play put on by the Earle Grey Players in a downtown Toronto church where . . . I was part of a crowd that had to scream, 'Crucify him! Crucify him!' I discovered that that was an outlet. I was a natural actor."

Findley wore his father's bedroom slippers in this first role. The slippers are not visible in a photograph taken during the performance, but the young actor's enthusiasm certainly is.

The group with which Findley made his acting début was established by Dublin-born actor and director Earle Grey in 1946. The Earle Grey Players performed for several summers in the Trinity College quadrangle in Toronto. The pay, Findley remembers, was $20 a week. With this company and the International Players, founded by Arthur Sutherland in 1948, Findley began his acting career. Looking back to his first roles, he sees that even then he had a need to engage in storytelling. Plays told stories; as an actor, Findley participated in their telling.

Speech and drama classes at the Royal Conservatory were added to ballet lessons while Findley worked at part-time jobs and took whatever acting roles he could get. Well-known Canadian actor William Hutt first met Findley when he gave the

FIGURE 4

*"Crucify him! Crucify him!" Timothy Findley (right) in his first acting
role, an Easter play, in 1948. He wore his father's bedroom slippers.*

young actor a part in a play he was directing, Sidney Howard's *The Silver Cord*. He recalls Findley as a very personable young man who walked onto the stage like a dancer. "He was a very intense student . . . for his age," Hutt told me. "He had an obvious dedication to acting."

Still plagued with poor health but, at twenty, eager for adventure, Findley went on a recuperative trip to Switzerland, paid for by his parents. He crossed the Atlantic on an ocean liner looking, in a photograph taken on the cruise, every inch the artistic young man from Rosedale.

After his return to Canada, Findley acted for radio and television. In a 1965 profile by June Graham, the CBC *Times* reported that Findley could not understand why he was often cast in comic roles, since, as he said, "I have no sense of humour to speak of." CBC producers, the profile adds, liked his highly intelligent, professional approach.

In 1952 he played the leading role of Peter Pupkin in the CBC's first television series, *Sunshine Sketches of a Little Town*, based on the stories of Canadian humorist Stephen Leacock. Findley recalls that he got the part quite by chance. He described to me how he had gone to the CBC office building on Jarvis Street to read for another part and after he had been politely thanked (clearly unsuccessful in getting the part) and was clattering down the staircase anxious to get away, producer Robert Allan called to him from overhead, "Mr. Findley, do you mind coming back for a moment?" Allan asked him to try reading the Peter Pupkin role. "I think," Allan said simply after hearing him read, "you should play this."

## STRATFORD

Findley's big acting break came in 1953 with the creation of a Shakespeare festival in nearby Stratford. Findley was invited to audition by Tyrone Guthrie who had seen him play Marchbanks in Bernard Shaw's *Candida*. When the Stratford company was

FIGURE 5

*Twenty-year-old Tiff Findley on his way
to Europe for a recuperative holiday.*

formed, Findley had parts in the inaugural season's two productions, playing Catesby in *Richard III* and a French officer in *All's Well That Ends Well*.

It was an exciting time in Canadian theatre when the actors assembled in Stratford that summer. Tyrone Guthrie came from England to direct the plays, bringing with him designer Tanya Moiseiwitsch, and actors Irene Worth and Alec Guinness. Many of Findley's colleagues that first season have become celebrated names in theatre, among them William Hutt, Douglas Campbell, Amelia Hall, William Needles, Douglas Rain, and Eric House. It was the glorious launching of a new era in Canadian theatre, not to mention a certain young actor's career.

That summer in Stratford was an exhilarating experience for Findley. He reminisced about it in an article called "Stratters, Ont." — Tyrone Guthrie's epithet for Stratford, Ontario, so as not to confuse it with the "real" Stratford in England. Findley recalled his first view of the thrust stage, designed by Guthrie and Moiseiwitsch to replicate the original style of Shakespearean theatres. After riding his bicycle beneath the maple trees along Ontario Street and across the Avon River, he arrived at a barn on the exhibition grounds for the first rehearsal:

A replica of the stage had been constructed there for us to work on. Our tented theatre was not yet in place. The very first day we all stood silent, staring at the mysterious structure with all its levels, steps and porches — wondering how to "get on board." None of us had ever seen a stage like that before. Its mystery and challenge were both alarming and magical.

Working with the famous director was a boon for a young actor, but it was also quite alarming. Findley describes one incident:

Director Tyrone Guthrie's mode of communication was unique. . . . Once, during a rehearsal, he was standing at the

FIGURE 6

*Preparing for the first rehearsal of the Stratford Festival's inaugural season in 1953. First row, from left: Irene Worth, Robert Goodier, Bruce Swerdfager, Amelia Hall. Second row, from left: Timothy Findley, Eric House, Roland Bull, Douglas Rain, Alex Smith, Betty Leighton. Third row, from left: William Needles, William Hutt, Robert Christie, Richard Robinson. Back row, seated: Elspeth Chisholm, John Hayes.*

furthest reaches of the house and he shouted down at the stage: "Findley! Not in China. Face making. Less. On!" Here's a translation: *Findley, I am not in China. Consequently, the message you are sending is overwhelming. Less face making, please. Proceed.*

In another rehearsal, Guthrie asked Findley to leap " 'blind' " from a centre-stage pillar, landing inches behind — but not on top of — Alec Guinness, the star of the festival. Findley perfected the jump, eliciting a collective gasp from the audience at every performance.

## TO LONDON: RUTH GORDON AND THORNTON WILDER

It was fortunate that Findley did not land on top of Alec Guinness because the British actor was so impressed with him and another young actor, Richard Easton, that he offered to pay their fares to England and provide accommodation and training at London's Central School of Speech and Drama. When the course was over, they were given parts in Guinness's West End production of *The Prisoner*. The play, written by Bridget Boland, is based loosely on the brainwashing torture suffered at the hands of Hungarian Communists by Cardinal Mindszenty. Alec Guinness played the Cardinal, Wilfrid Lawson, his jailer, and Findley, a clerk in the office of the prosecutor. Findley felt certain his star was rising. There he was in London, the heart of the theatre world, learning his craft with the best actors in the world and having a fabulous time.

For the next three years Findley worked as a contract actor with H.M. Tennent, London's most prolific theatrical producer. One of his roles was the snobbish waiter Rudolph in Tyrone Guthrie's production of Thornton Wilder's well-known play, *The Matchmaker*, at London's famous Haymarket Theatre. Once again, Findley had the good fortune to work with, and impress, illustrious theatre people. During *The Matchmaker*'s long run, he became friends with Ruth Gordon, who played Dolly Levi in the production, and through her with playwright Thornton Wilder. These two people were instrumental in recognizing and encouraging Findley's true vocation; their association with him marked a turning point in his life.

Findley often tells how Ruth Gordon provided the impetus for his first short story when *The Matchmaker* was on tour. This is how he told the story to Alison Summers:

We had been to an exhibition of paintings in Manchester, all done by people under thirty years of age. . . . When we came out, Ruth asked me "Why are you[ng] people so damned negative about everything? All those pictures were black, depressing, ugly. Can't you say *yes* to anything?" . . . Secretly I decided, "I'll prove that we're not." I went back to my digs and I wrote a story. I didn't have a typewriter, so I wrote it out again by hand and gave it to her. It was a story called "About Effie," about one of the maids who worked at our house when I was a kid. The next day I got word from Ruth's dresser to go and see her. Ruth was sitting in the room crying, and she threw her arms around me and said, "Oh Tiffy, you really shouldn't be acting at all; you should be writing." (Which is a lovely thing to be told when you want to be an actor.) . . . [She] had my story typed. . . . Then [she] showed it to Thornton Wilder.

After reading the story, Wilder suggested that Findley write a play. He did so, and several weeks later, after it had been delivered and duly read by Wilder, Findley answered the master playwright's summons to come to his suite at the Savoy Hotel to discuss it. He describes his preparations and Wilder's verdict in *Inside Memory*:

I had, as every actor had, an audition suit. Blue. Somewhat baggy — but presentable. Late Sunday afternoon, I dressed for my "audition" for the Master. I polished my shoes and borrowed a better tie than the one I owned and I looked many hours at myself in the mirror. . . .

Up from Tedworth Square, along Royal Hospital Road and then up to Sloane Square Station. I am going to Charing Cross on the Circle Line. None of my precautions are working. My stomach churns with apprehension — my blue suit shines with a dreadful gloss beneath the lights — my hair, which is cut in the Junker's style for my role in the play, is standing on end and crackling with electricity. My palms are sweating and my feet are cold. I have all the sophistication of a spotted disease.

Wilder opened the door just as Findley knocked, and, after the young man fell into the room, colliding with the master, Wilder ordered Findley a large meal. While the hungry young actor ate filet mignon, roast potatoes, and shrimps on ice, the playwright paced up and down the room with scotch and cigarettes and proceeded to rip Findley's first play to shreds:

"Be confident," he said, "that whatever I say is said as one writer to another. I do not mince words — but neither do I mince writers. You are a writer, Findley. That's a certainty. What you have written, on the other hand. . . ."

Wilder allowed that Findley could write dialogue and admitted that some of his images were good, but he found little else to praise. He advised the young actor/writer to put the play away in a drawer — to keep it as a reminder of how good intentions go awry — and to try again, something that was not imitative, something written in his own voice.

Thornton Wilder became Findley's friend and mentor until his death in 1975. In *Inside Memory*, Findley describes their many "pub crawls" and endless talks about theatre and literature. Late one night in London, gazing up at the massive doors of St. Paul's Cathedral, they excitedly devised a staging of *Agamemnon* on the

FIGURE 7

*The* Hamlet *tour actors boarding the* DC-10 *to Moscow.*
*From left to right: Diana Wynyard, Ernest Thesiger, Paul Scofield,*
*Alec Clunes, Mary Ure, Timothy Findley, and Gerald Flood.*

cathedral's steps. Wilder's infectious delight in spontaneous moments like this one is Findley's fondest memory of the famous playwright who encouraged his first attempts at writing.

First a celebrated actress and then a famous playwright tell Findley that he is a writer. What better encouragement could a young man have to pursue a career in writing?

How did Findley feel about his acting career? Why did he follow his mentors' advice and continue writing? In a 1967 CBC Television interview he told Warren Davis that he had discovered a unique voice in his writing which he realized he could not express by acting roles created by other writers. There was another reason too. Findley told me that he began to feel "boxed in," trapped in the minor roles he was given. "I felt stuck, playing very small roles and it made me terribly unhappy. When you're young you think that you're worth more, you can do more, you can do anything." The minor role he was playing in *The Matchmaker* "seemed to go on forever." Findley would get calls for other plays, but Ruth Gordon wanted to keep the company intact. The producer bowed to her strong will and no one was released. For month after month, in London and on tour, Findley played the angry and arrogant Rudolph, a role that allowed little variation and less scope.

### ''UNFORGETTABLE JOURNEY''

Finally free of *The Matchmaker*, in 1955 Findley played the role of Osric in Peter Brook's production of *Hamlet* at London's Phoenix Theatre. The company, which included Paul Scofield, Diana Wynyard, Alec Clunes, Mary Ure, and Ernest Thesiger, was invited to Moscow as the first English-speaking acting group to perform in the Soviet Union since before the 1917 revolution. In "An Unforgettable Journey to Russia," Findley describes the final Lithuania-Moscow stage of the long and harrowing flight in an ancient DC-10 — an experience that he admits contributed to his fear of flying:

Increasingly, as the flight wore on, it became apparent that we really were in trouble. It became very cold in the plane. Everyone put on an overcoat. Blankets were offered. The pilot was attempting to climb above the storm, but he was failing to achieve his goal. The snow, apparently, went all the way to heaven.

Nobody spoke, which is the way of people in jeopardy, it seems. Neighbours retreated into private thoughts. We turned very slightly away from one another. The DC-10 began to shake and shudder. I thought how young we all were — even Ernest in his seventies. It is always too soon to die, I guess.

The plane landed safely despite the storm and *Hamlet* was a great success. As the Canadian of the group, Findley was asked by Herbert Whittaker, theatre critic for the Toronto *Globe and Mail*, to write about his experience. After praising the Russians' flamboyant acting style and the crew's careful attention to production details, Findley wrote that the tragedy of Russian theatre is that " 'propaganda is the one tongue. They lack that freedom which we have, which is, that we may tell what truth we are moved to tell and not that only which is expedient to be told.' " This was Findley's first public expression of his creed as a creative artist. His experience in the Soviet Union had indeed left a deep impression. Findley subsequently became an outspoken critic of the censorship and oppression of writers and other artists. He holds sacred the right of artists to tell the truth as they see it; it is, he believes, their duty.

## "TIFFY HAS BEEN PUBLISHED"

Findley returned to North America in 1956, rejoining *The Matchmaker* for the remainder of its New York engagement and a cross-country tour. During the New York run, "About Effie," the short story that Ruth Gordon had inspired, was published in the first issue of a new Canadian literary magazine, *Tamarack Review*, and Findley received a copy in the mail. He often tells the story of Gordon's fury after he barged impulsively into her dressing room to show her his first published story. As he told me, "She was, to put it mildly, incompletely dressed. Her anger at my intrusion was spectacular." Half-an-hour later, as the curtain was about to rise on the next act, he was forced back into her presence. In his memoir, he tells of Gordon's announcement to the assembled cast:

> Since everyone is in this scene, the whole company is now assembled. Ruth will come — and fire me in front of all my friends.
>
> She sweeps out onto the stage. The curtain is down. We can hear the audience.
>
> "Listen, everybody!" Ruth says. "I have something to tell you all about Mister Findley. . . ."
>
> Oh, God.
>
> She turns towards me and smiles. The whole shebang. She has the kind of smile that kills.
>
> "Darlin'," she says. "I want them all to know."
>
> Then she turns and says to the others: "Tiffy has been published! And here it is, in my hand."
>
> She shows the magazine and turns back to me and pulls me down and kisses me on the top of my head.
>
> "Next time you're published, darlin' — I only hope I'm stark naked!"

Findley wrote two more short stories during the late 1950s that were later published, "War" and "The Name's the Same," as well as several more that were not, but which formed a necessary part of the young writer's development.

And he continued to act. How good an actor was Findley? Could he have had a successful stage career? Jean Roberts, who worked with Findley early on, remarked to Elspeth Cameron that he had the potential to be a second William Hutt. In the same article, however, actor and director Marigold Charlesworth

FIGURE 8

*The young actor at the time he went to Hollywood;*
*acting jobs in television and movies were hard to find.*

noted that he was always terribly nervous, a "butterflies-in-the-stomach actor." William Hutt told me that he found Findley's performances at Stratford "very fine," but he remembers having a vague feeling that acting was not really his *"tasse du thé"*: "I watched his performance and thought, yes, it's good, he has a presence on the stage. But there was something stiff about him, not physical but mental stiffness, a reluctance to share or perhaps a fear of sharing." Findley's own assessment, as recounted to Alison Summers, is that "I was a good actor — I could have had a career. I'd never have been a star, not in a thousand years, but I would always have been a useful actor, a good second string — which in a sense is the best thing to be, because you do go on forever. . . ." Luckily for Canadian literature, Timothy Findley did not go on acting forever.

## HOLLYWOOD

In 1956 *The Matchmaker* tour came to an end in California. Findley stayed on in Hollywood, the mecca of movies and television, but his experience there helped convince him that his future lay in writing rather than on the stage. There were many actors looking for work and few acting jobs to be had, so he scraped together enough to live on by doing odd jobs and modelling.

In Hollywood he again had the valuable friendship of Ruth Gordon, and her husband Garson Kanin. Together they introduced Tiff to other young performers and various television and film people, taking him to restaurants where Hedda Hopper or Jimmy Stewart were likely to drop by their table. One evening at Romanoff's, "the great place to be," as Findley puts it, Ruth slipped him an envelope under the table. In it were five postdated cheques, each for $100 (a good deal of money in those days), so that he could stop looking for acting jobs and get on with his writing. She also introduced him to Stanley Colbert, who became Findley's agent. Colbert and his wife Nancy were more than literary agents, as it turned out — they were life-supporters. Findley found himself babysitting their infant daughter and joining their "crazy, wondrous, joyful, disastrous and immensely creative household of crippled, recovering actors and writers — of whom I was one. . . ." In *Inside Memory*, he continues his description of life in Hollywood:

I had been writing a novel — living in Santa Monica with three inverted artists (one of whom painted in the nude) and I had been making my living working as a model in the life class at U.C.L.A.

My food had consisted of dried Lipton's soup, from which — if you used a strainer to contain the solids in the mix — you could get about three tasteless meals of coloured water. I also collected ripe avocados from the front yard of other houses on the street, and revelled in the sense of utter nourishment they gave. My other food was cigarettes and bottles of Thunderbird wine, which you could buy for seventy-five cents apiece.

Findley, ever the storyteller, makes his eighteen months in Hollywood sound amusing, but the reality was perhaps more grim. The Hollywood reflected in his 1969 novel, *The Butterfly Plague*, is a nightmare world of fire and rape, a world where " 'the perfection of gesture' " has become a menace. Findley was painfully aware of the underside of Hollywood's glamour. He was drinking heavily, often depressed, and struggling to find his way in an overpopulated, hostile environment.

In the Hollywood home of screenwriter Ivan Moffat, Findley made a chance discovery that would alter his life and work. Left on his own and told to make himself at home, he casually opened a book of photographs. The pictures, taken by Moffat as the first official photographer allowed through the gates of the Nazi concentration camp at Dachau, were more graphic and horrific than any seen by the public up to that time. Findley described his reaction to them in a speech, "My Final Hour":

I was looking into hell — and hell was real.

And I saw all this in *Hollywood, California* — high above the magic of its lights and the perfume of its heady scent and I saw it through the sound of someone singing: *"I get no kick from cocaine . . . mere alcohol doesn't thrill me at all. . . ."*

I never recovered from what I saw that night.

Perhaps I should say: thank God. I cannot tell.

But, at least, I had been joined — through a unique revelation of horror — to the rest of the human race. I was never to see myself again as a being apart. How, after all, can you be *apart* when everyone else is standing *apart* beside you?

This was a kind of epiphany. I did not know how to say it then, but the vision of Dachau in Ivan Moffat's photographs told me that I was just like everyone else. We are all a collective hiding place for monsters.


Findley did use Ruth Gordon's gift to support his writing while he was in Hollywood, producing what he had to agree with the Colberts was a dreadful novel. They burned it together in the fireplace.

A few months after having returned to Toronto, Findley made a second trip to Hollywood, this time with a writing job in hand. Early in 1958, Stanley Colbert phoned to tell him that the prestigious television drama series *Playhouse 90* was interested in producing a play based on Findley's short story, "Lemonade." While he was in Hollywood working on the script, the studio would give him a job doctoring other scripts — rewriting scenes, creating new scenes, scripting lines of dialogue. Findley was elated, but after a few short months *Playhouse 90* produced another play dealing with alcoholism, J.P. Miller's *Days of Wine and Roses*. Not wanting to do two plays on the same topic that season, the producers summarily dismissed Findley. He described the incident to me as one of the many times in his early life when things seemed to be going well, but suddenly "a car came veering out of nowhere and ran me down." Findley's dream of becoming a famous scriptwriter ended abruptly, and he returned to Toronto, depressed and discouraged.

Living in Los Angeles the second time, however, had one positive result. It convinced Findley that he did not want to spend the rest of his life living in a city. In a 1971 CBC *Matinee* radio broadcast, he described his revelation this way:

> there I was walking along whatever street it was, having just come out of one concrete monstrosity, passing by others and heading for the one I worked in. Little plastic trees had been set up in tubs at intervals along the sidewalk. And as I made my way, I looked down at my feet and then up at the invisible sky, and was aware of the concrete that hedged me in — and I thought: but I wasn't born into *this*. My *body* wasn't born into this . . . *place*! I was born *alive*; yet this is where I'm asking my body to function.

The people he passed on the streets, worked with, bought his groceries from, were impersonal, cold; he would never know them nor would they know him. He describes his closest relationship — with a fly:

> No kidding. This fly and I lived together for almost three months, until one day he got drowned in the tin shower-stall — and I have often thought about that and been reasonably certain it was suicide. I was so fond of that fly I actually wept. And in a dream I thought I found his little towel and six neatly matched tiny slippers at the edge of the shower and a note that read, "This is for the best, Tiff. City life is not for me. Good luck from your best friend, Buzz." I left Los Angeles shortly after that, saying to myself, "This is for the best, Buzz — city life is not for me."

This second stay in Hollywood also convinced Findley that he did not want to remain in the movie business. He saw how stars were treated — fawned upon and despised at the same time —

how competition and rivalry were so intense that actors would virtually kill each other for a role. Findley portrayed this aspect of Hollywood in *The Butterfly Plague*, in which movie producer George Damarosch's motto is " 'Don't give 'em what they want, make 'em want what you've got.' " But there was also a positive side to Findley's Hollywood experience: watching the talented *Playhouse 90* actors and directors work on the many excellent productions. And the screen-writing experience, though limited to other writers' scripts, was invaluable.

## A BRIEF MARRIAGE

Acting jobs were more plentiful in Toronto when Findley arrived home in 1958. Canadian television was just getting established and actors and scriptwriters were in demand. He appeared in adaptations of works by Charles Dickens, Anton Chekhov, and Jean Anouilh — as well as in several Canadian works — on CBC Radio and Television.

In a television drama called *Sanctuary*, Findley played a soldier wounded in the War of 1812 who is helped by a blind girl unaware that he is one of the enemy. An actress from Winnipeg, Janet Reid, played the blind girl, and despite Findley's professed homosexuality, they fell in love and were married, trusting that somehow things would work out. Things didn't work out. The brief marriage was annulled after a humiliating court appearance. He and Janet Reid remained friends but the courtroom experience was devastating to Findley. He had been told by the judge that as a homosexual he was "not a man" — an acceptable epithet in those days, even in a court of law.

A terrible time followed. Findley would wake up in strange hotel rooms, unable to remember how or with whom he had arrived. Friends received desperate calls in the middle of night. A series of psychiatric sessions did little to alleviate the dark visions, the doubts and insecurities. But Findley continued writing, working on his early novels and receiving occasional

FIGURE 9

*Timothy Findley as a soldier wounded in the*
*War of 1812 and Janet Reid as the blind girl who helps*
*him in* Sanctuary. *They were briefly married.*

assignments for radio scripts from CBC producers, such as Robert Weaver, Beverley Roberts, and James Anderson, who recognized his talent.

## MEETS BILL WHITEHEAD

It was William Whitehead who finally stopped Findley's slide into despair. They met in 1962 when Findley acted in a repertory season coproduced by Whitehead.

Bill Whitehead took an unusual route to the theatre. At the University of Saskatchewan he studied biology, earning two degrees. For his Master's thesis, *The Musculature of the Black Widow Spider*, he raised, as Findley puts it, "three thousand of the little poisoners." When the Canadian Players visited Saskatoon, Whitehead went to a performance — his first live-theatre experience — and was enchanted. He decided then and there to quit science and become an actor. By 1962 he had teamed up with Jean Roberts and Marigold Charlesworth to produce a unique series of plays in repertory at Toronto's Central Library during the winter and at the Red Barn Theatre in Jackson's Point, Ontario, in the summer. Findley was hired as one of the original company. Whitehead and Findley appeared on stage together only once, when an actor in *The Rivals* died suddenly and Bill had to take his place.

It has become an amusing story now, but the friendship got off to a shaky start. The first time Whitehead invited Findley over, he had enough money for either beer or food and opted for the beer, based on what he knew of Findley's reputation for drink. A hungry Findley arrived, unable to drink the beer because he had just taken Antabuse, a drug that would make him violently ill if he consumed alcohol. Despite its inauspicious beginning, the friendship survived and prospered; in fact, Findley and Whitehead have been together ever since. Findley has said he was nearly incapacitated by alcohol until he met Bill and discovered there was something that made sobriety worth striving

FIGURE 10

*The Rivals: the only time that Findley and Bill Whitehead*
*appeared together on stage. "I was producing the play and the*
*other actor died, so I had to play the part," recalls Whitehead.*

for. Findley has always been candid about the part alcohol has played in his life.

Their first summer together, Findley and Whitehead rented an empty house in Richmond Hill that Findley's parents had bought as a retirement home. Both men retired from the theatre and devoted themselves to writing for radio and television. Findley first got a job writing advertising copy for CFGM, Richmond Hill's country-and-western radio station. With his biology degrees, Whitehead was hired to write the science news for CBC Radio's *The Learning Stage* (forerunner to *Ideas*), and later Findley wrote the arts news for the same program. He remembers it as " 'an absolutely marvellous job.' " He enjoyed covering art exhibits, plays, and concerts, and discovered a new way of writing. " 'Out of the experience,' " he told David MacFarlane, " 'came a lot of what might be called my style — the use of interview as a basis for narrative, the chop shots, getting into things quickly and then getting out. I had magically fallen on my feet with a way that worked.' "

In addition to writing for radio and television, Findley composed most of his first novel, *The Last of the Crazy People*, in the Richmond Hill garden. While Findley pursued fiction, Whitehead continued to write for television. In the course of his career, Whitehead wrote many award-winning documentaries, including over one hundred episodes for *The Nature of Things*.

## STONE ORCHARD

In 1964, while looking for a house in the country that would provide the quiet and isolation Findley needed in order to write, the pair discovered their future home, Stone Orchard. A limited budget — $3000 for a down payment — and a range within a fifty-mile radius of Toronto-based publishing and broadcasting opportunities, restricted their search. But one day they got lost northeast of Toronto and discovered a dilapidated brick farmhouse with fifty acres of rolling fields near the small town of

FIGURE II

*Findley and his dogs, shortly after moving to Stone*
*Orchard: "I could not have found a better place to live."*

Cannington. It was twenty miles outside their limit, but at $9000, well within their budget.

Findley felt spiritually drawn to that part of Ontario, not far from where his great-grandparents had settled in the 1840s and his grandfather Thomas Findley had delivered the mail on horseback. He felt he had come home. As he says in the National Film Board documentary, looking out over the farm, "This whole world of rolling land and the trees, the feel of this earth; it is literally where I feel my feet belong and it is a place filled with magic."

The original three-bedroom house was built in 1848 by Alfie Wyatt, a young English chemist who served the nearby villages of Derryville and Ellis's Corners from a pharmacy in what is now the dining room. Wyatt expanded the house in 1870, adding a brick extension for his married son, and moved his shop to Cannington. Over the years, Findley and Whitehead have made considerable improvements to the house, including extra bedrooms, a greenhouse, and a bright and spacious second-floor addition that serves as Findley's unique bedroom, study, and retreat. The entire house is filled with books, plants, artwork, antiques, heirlooms, and memorabilia. Many pieces are from the Findley and Whitehead families, others were found over the years at auctions or "inherited" from friends — all displayed in Victorian profusion. First-time visitors find it hard to concentrate on the conversation; there are so many fascinating things to look at.

Findley has a story for nearly every object. He describes the small red sofa that Grandfather Bull had built in his piano factory as an anniversary gift for his wife, the pewter picture frames Bill's mother made on the prairies in Depression times, his mother's writing desk converted from a spinet piano, the brass lamps that produce the kind of warm glow that Findley so often describes in his writing, and the pump organ from the vanished church in Derryville, once a thriving community just down the road. These pieces, says Findley, connect him and Bill to the past. "They are inheritances that, every time we look at them, tell us who we are," he explained to me. "The important thing is not that they are very old or finely-made pieces, but the people, the story, behind them."

In front of the house is a stone wall that has a story Bill Whitehead loves to tell. He related it once again for my benefit:

When we were building the stone wall, it occurred to us that we should put in a sort of time capsule. We found some coins and wrote a note describing what kind of day it was, who we were, how much we'd loved living here and we named the current heads of state and the world news. The notes were modelled on similar information that had been written on a beam in our barn in 1901. We wanted to put them in a Coke bottle (having said in the notes that Coke was the salient product of our time) but the coins wouldn't fit through the neck of the bottle. "Quick! The mortar's drying!" a workman shouted. So Tiff ran into the house and got a mayonnaise jar. Whoever discovers it will think we were pretty weird Coke drinkers (*the wide-mouth Coke culture of the '70s*), because we didn't have time to change the reference to Coke bottles in the note.

The property is called Stone Orchard after *The Cherry Orchard* by Anton Chekhov, a playwright Findley admires. He can envision scenes of that play taking place in the house's stately rooms. But there were no cherries when they bought the farm, and the only field crop they could identify with certainty was stones. Hence, Stone Orchard.

They later discovered that their choice of Stone Orchard as a name had been a bit of a joke in the area: in local slang, a *stone orchard* is a cemetery. If at first Cannington residents had a chuckle at the newcomers' naïveté, were curious about the bohemian artists from the city, and cautious about two men keeping house together, they have come to accept Findley and Whitehead as "the boys" and consider them a part of their community. For their part, "the boys" have come to respect and love their neighbours. " 'The people here are fabulous,' " Whitehead told Catherine Dunphy. " 'Neighbor is a verb. You are judged on how you neighbor.' " Findley says simply: "I could not have found a better place to live."

Findley had found his home at Stone Orchard and his companion in Bill Whitehead. With them came the peace and security he needed to pursue his writing. Whitehead is a steadying, nurturing presence for Findley. He looks after the practical side of their life together, acting as chauffeur (Findley does not drive), domestic manager (his Swedish meatballs are superb), and secretary (transforming Tiff's "atrocious" handwriting into neatly word-processed manuscripts). As an experienced writer himself, Whitehead is also Findley's first editor. He explained to Judith Fitzgerald:

> "Tiff is a great writer, but he does tend to get stopped at walls and doors in his work. Sometimes we read his manuscripts together to see where he's stuck. He gets caught in perfection and tends to digress so much that the plot gets away from him. I guess I'm his first editor that way, because if it gets by me, it's got to be okay."

The two writers share opinions, jokes, ideas, and crossword puzzles; their affection and respect for each other is obvious to even a casual acquaintance.

## FILM WORK

During the late 1960s, Findley wrote extensively for CBC Radio and Television — profiles of actors Kate Reid and William Hutt and director Michael Langham, documentaries on theatre companies, a series of interviews with writers, an offbeat Easter drama called *Who Crucified Christ?*, and *The Paper People*, CBC's first feature-length colour film, coproduced with the National Film Board.

When it was broadcast in December 1967, *The Paper People* caused an uproar. Members of parliament joined the public and critics in an outcry over the film's subject matter and $300,000 production cost. The film features an artist named Jamie Taylor who constructs life-size figures out of papier-mâché (the paper people), sets them on fire in a junk yard, and films the conflagration, creating with their destruction "disposable art." Film director David Gardner described disposable art as the reflection of the materialistic world coming to an end, where the only permanence is impermanence, where everything is disposable. Findley came up with the plot idea after producer Mervyn Rosenzveig said he wanted a script that would capture the essence of the political and social upheavals of the 1960s. Jamie Taylor's life and art do just that.

In the original version of the script, Jamie Taylor was a photographer, but after Findley saw Michelangelo Antonioni's film *Blow-Up*, he changed the photographer to an artist to avoid the obvious comparisons. *The Paper People* has a film-within-a-film structure; a woman film-maker sets out to make a documentary about the artist, who has become newsworthy because of his unique disposable-art gimmick. Her story frames Jamie's.

The CBC wanted the script completed quickly, and Findley needed the $3,000 they offered him. A writer continually works under deadlines, but the pressure exerted by the National Film Board was extreme. Findley received a daily phone call: "How many pages have you written?" they would ask. When Findley submitted the completed script, the director, producer, and script editor took over. They each had a further hand in shaping the script before and during filming.

The following year, Findley wrote a script for another film, *Don't Let the Angels Fall*. Once again the angst of the 1960s was the subject, this time centring on an urban family trying to cope with changes in social and moral values. The film opened at the 1969 Cannes Festival but inspired hardly a ripple of critical or popular interest.

Working on these films was extremely frustrating for Findley. After painstakingly creating the script, he had to stand by and watch it be radically adapted to others' ideas. This was especially true of *Don't Let the Angels Fall*; he barely recognized the finished film. Writing fiction, on the other hand, was a solitary act that allowed him to express his vision without collaboration or compromise. In this medium, Findley was writer, actor, and director all at once.

### EARLY NOVELS: *THE LAST OF THE CRAZY PEOPLE*

Although fiction is Findley's most natural creative medium, writing does not come to him easily. He spoke to fellow writer Graeme Gibson about the loneliness of writing and of the difficulty of living with his characters as he struggles to get them down on paper:

> You're intellectually lonely: no one — hardly anyone "understands" you, because your whole life — maybe I should say your whole *existence* is an intensified searching — not for your own identity — but for your *work's* identity. And this intellectual loneliness leads to your being emotionally cut off. It isn't merely eccentricity of spirit, you know, that makes so many of us seek the "red corners" of our lives — or that so many of us drink. . . . [W]ho wants to spend their life alone with a lot of maniacs screaming: "Let me out of your mind!"?

But Findley soon discovered that writing his first two novels, however agonizing, was easier than getting them published. For three years the manuscript of *The Last of the Crazy People* made the rounds of Canadian publishers and was repeatedly rejected. One publisher indignantly insisted that nothing like Hooker's story could ever happen in Canada.

The novel is about eleven-year-old Hooker Winslow who sees the despair and isolation of the other members of his family and concludes that there is only one way to save them. Findley explained to Donald Cameron how it came about that Hooker's story ends as it does:

> It evolved absolutely against my will: one night I was upstairs writing and came down in floods of tears because I had discovered that this was the only thing that he could do. You would imagine, I'm sure, that the book had been written from the very first word in the knowledge that that was what was going to happen — it wasn't. At first I thought that perhaps he went downstairs into the cellar and killed his cats, and then about two days after that I realized that that isn't what he did, that he had to save the family by ending their lives, ending their misery.

This story reveals something of Findley's method of writing. The plot often evolves in unexpected and even undesired ways, and the characters behave according to their own intentions rather than Findley's.

As Hooker's story took shape on the page, Findley recalled a forgotten experience from his past that had perhaps unconsciously guided him toward the novel's tragic ending. As he told Graeme Gibson:

> In the true story there was a child who killed one of his parents and one sister and one other person who happened to be in the house, and made an attempt on the other lives in the house, but failed. Then he went, as Hooker does, into the hospital and suffered; but ultimately, in real life he emerged. And I was thunderstuck by what I considered the beauty, in the sense of the simplicity, of his statement when someone . . . said to him: Can you tell me why you did it? He said: Because I loved them so.

*The Last of the Crazy People* does have a survivor, one of Findley's several similar characters, a woman with a strong hold on reality who accepts life's pain and carries on. Iris Browne, the Winslows' black maid for thirty years, practises acceptance and resignation. She has outlived her parents, her brothers and sisters, and her cousins. Although her father forbade his children to become servants, Iris works as a maid, having discovered that the real enemy is poverty. Like Bertha Millroy in "Lemonade," Iris is modelled on the maids who kept young Tiff company in the Findleys' Rosedale kitchen.

In the United States, where it was published in 1967, the novel sold moderately well and won critical praise. Margaret Parton, writing in the prestigious *Saturday Review*, stated that she could not recommend the book as light summer reading, but affirmed that it "says something important, and says it with both craftsmanship and compassion." In Canada, it sold poorly. Critics complained that it relied too much on the southern Gothic tradition. Robert Fulford found Hooker's story "unrelieved gloom." Findley's writing skills were consistently praised, however, and J.M. Stedmond declared, "Findley's is a talent to keep an eye on."

## EARLY NOVELS: *THE BUTTERFLY PLAGUE*

When his next manuscript was finished and again rejected by Canadian presses, Findley took the train to New York to see an American publisher. He arrived the day before his appointment and, having calmed his frayed nerves with several beers on the train, continued to drink in his hotel room. Morning and the appointed hour arrived, and Findley managed to call a taxi. With the precious yellow pages of the manuscript in an open box on his lap, they pulled up in front of the publisher's building. Out of the cab, unsteadily searching for his forgotten wallet, the wind lifted the loose pages from the box and. . . . In his memoirs, Findley continues one of his favourite New York stories:

A nightmare ensued. . . .
Tiddly Irish cabby and drunk Timothy Findley and half a dozen wind-blown passers-by all rushed after yellow pages

— leaping — running — falling down. Looking up, all I could see was a whirlwind of yellow — giving way, as one draught fought against another over Madison Avenue — so that pages rose on one side and fell on the other. Traffic was halted. People, being kind, went through balletic exertions — and, at last, the manuscript was retrieved entirely and the lid clamped down on the box.

The editor was not impressed with Findley's condition — nor with that of the manuscript — when he eventually arrived in her office with the cabby (who hadn't yet been paid) and a crumpled bundle of yellow pages. In fact, she kicked him out. However, Bill Whitehead soon arrived and fences were mended. *The Butterfly Plague*, Findley's second novel, was released by Viking Press in the spring of 1969.

Dreamlike, inventive, and rich in symbolism, the novel is set in the 1930s in Hollywood and Hitler's Germany and links the movie-world's rage for physical perfection with fascist ideals. The plot centres on the Damarosch family: George, a film director planning his comeback; Naomi, a star of the silent screen dying of cancer; Adolphus, their haemophiliac son; and daughter Ruth, a former Olympic swimmer who married her coach in Nazi Germany. Central to the book's theme is Naomi's warning to her daughter: " 'the greatest flaw of all, the very worst, the most destructive and the seat of all our woes and pain, is this *dream* — this damnable quest for perfection.' "

Findley had been on such a quest since his early days as a dancer. Had he come to realize that to follow this path to its ultimate conclusion was to embrace a kind of fascist idealism? It was in Hollywood, remember, that he saw the Dachau photographs and came face-to-face with the horrors of the Nazi regime. In the novel there is a clear parallel between Ruth's search for spiritual perfection and the Nazi ideal of racial purity. Fascism was to become a central theme in Findley's writing.

*The Butterfly Plague* was virtually ignored in Canada. Only two reviews were published, both written by fellow writer Marian

Engel and published in two Toronto newspapers. She applauded the book in one review and damned it in the other. In the *Star*, she praised Findley's "conversational manner" and ability to handle difficult material "with delicacy and humor." For the *Telegram*, on the other hand, she wrote that the novel was "fey and empty at the core." In a special issue of *Room of One's Own* devoted to Marian Engel, Findley tells the story of their first encounter, at an early meeting of the Writers' Union:

> You can see my dilemma. As I have, since, seen Marian Engel's dilemma. Writing reviews was one of the very few ways a writer could supplement income, in those days. And — after all — she was probably the only Canadian who had ever read — let alone heard of — *The Butterfly Plague*. The thing is, I didn't care at all that she had reviewed it twice: what I didn't like was that in one of those reviews, she'd had the temerity to suggest it wasn't the greatest thing ever written. That it was "okay — but. . . ." Well, anyway — I was alarmed at the prospect of meeting her. And, there in the Jorgenson gallery — stirring her cup — she said something like: "Hi. You're Findley, aren't you. I suppose you want to shoot me."

He didn't — in fact, they become close friends. The reviews, and their first encounter, became a fond joke between them.

## "THE JOURNEY"

Findley and Bill Whitehead spent the summer of 1969 on a journey that led them into Canada's northern wilderness. Starting at their traditional holiday spot, the Atlantic House Hotel in Maine, they drove west across the United States with a kayak and camping gear strapped onto the roof of their old Citroen. Heading north into Canada, they camped at Glacier National Park, kayaked up the Peace River, and finally arrived at Wood Buffalo Park, which straddles the border of Alberta and the Northwest

Territories. In this setting Findley came to realize how deeply affected he was by the natural world and how absolutely the human spirit is rooted in the earth. In "The Journey," a radio play based on the trip, the narrator describes his moment of discovery:

> We were camped by a lake — perhaps the most beautiful lake I've ever seen, up in Wood Buffalo Park. In the morning, we would head back. So, that night, I went outside by myself and I just stood, watching the lake and the sky and its late sunset — until, slowly, but absolutely, I was overcome by some pathetic yearning and I was overcome, simultaneously, with a terrible sense of loss and sorrow. It was as if something had died, or had been permanently lost — not just to me but to everyone, forever. And I thought of the animals there and of the birds and the fish and even of the insects. . . . And I knew that I was no better and no worse — no larger and no smaller than any other creature that walks or crawls or flies or swims. I'm merely different.

It was, Bill Whitehead told me, the best summer of their lives.

Back at Stone Orchard and writing again, Findley grew increasingly despondent over the lack of recognition his work had garnered in his own country. The Bantam edition of *The Butterfly Plague* did not even acknowledge that he was a Canadian, and Macmillan Publishers in Toronto, distributors of the Canadian edition, kept forwarding his mail to New York, apparently unaware that he lived nearby.

A troubled time followed as Findley again plunged into doubt and despair, drinking heavily. For a time he left Cannington to work in New England on a filmscript for *The Last of the Crazy People* that was never produced. Away from the stability of Stone Orchard, his life fell apart. In New York, the day he was supposed to catch a train to return home, he accidentally locked himself into the apartment of an old friend where he was staying. He had gotten so drunk he could not undo the lock; someone on the outside had to break down the door in order to let Findley out. "Funny only in retrospect," he told me. His return to Stone Orchard and Bill Whitehead's presence ended the crisis.


## WRITING FOR TELEVISION

Frustrated by the poor reception of his novels and in need of income, in the 1970s Findley turned increasingly to television writing. His scripts for *The Whiteoaks of Jalna*, a family saga based on the novels of Mazo de la Roche, are among his best-known work for television. The twelve-part series was broadcast in 1972, and although some reviewers predicted great success, critical and popular reception was lukewarm.

Another series, a collaboration with Bill Whitehead, was an unqualified success. *The National Dream*, based on Pierre Berton's book and starring William Hutt as Sir John A. Macdonald, chronicled the building of the Canadian Pacific Railway. Among the Timothy Findley Papers in the National Archives of Canada are the outlines, scripts, and research material for the series, including lengthy memoranda from Pierre Berton. A stickler for accurate historical detail, Berton often commented on details of speech or dress in the preliminary scripts.

In one scene, Findley had invented a pair of white kid gloves for Sir John A. — gloves that the prime minister disliked wearing and lost at every opportunity. As Findley told me, Berton penned him a note saying: "Nothing in my research informs me that Sir John A. Macdonald had an aversion to white kid gloves. Please remove all references to same." But Findley needed the gloves as an important piece of comic business in a scene involving Sir John A. and his wife. He decided to talk to Donald Creighton — noted Canadian historian and Macdonald biographer — in an attempt to defend his position. Having put the dilemma before the historian, Findley was delighted when Creighton produced a photograph of Sir John A. in evening dress — barehanded. "Now," Creighton had said, "if that doesn't prove his aversion to white kid gloves — what does?"

Meanwhile, Berton had talked to actor William Hutt about the problem. Hutt convinced Berton that the gloves were useful to the scene and perhaps not so terribly important historically. Findley was only sorry that Hutt's persuasiveness had trumped Creighton's brilliant solution.

Findley and Whitehead won an ACTRA Award for *The National Dream* in 1975.

## RETURN TO THE THEATRE

Findley was well on the way to becoming a successful writer for radio and television, but he longed to return to live theatre — as a playwright. In 1974 the National Arts Centre gave him that opportunity when it appointed him its first playwright-in-residence. To learn the craft of playwriting and staging, Findley was hired to follow the day-to-day production of John Coulter's *Riel*, currently being rehearsed at the NAC. He took with him to Ottawa the beginning of his own script and applied to it what he was learning about theatre production.

The result, *Can You See Me Yet?*, was staged at the National Arts Centre the following year. Frances Hyland played Cassandra Wakelin, an inmate of an Ontario asylum for the insane in 1938, on the eve of World War II. The psychodrama explored the loveless, stultifying Wakelin family and its contribution to Cassandra's breakdown. Each actor in the drama played a dual role: a member of the Wakelin family and an inmate of the asylum, one character mirrored in the other.

In the article "Alice Drops Her Cigarette on the Floor . . . ," Findley described how he rewrote the play in order to be true to his characters:

> I wrote it all first as a straightforward play about a family: the family of Cassandra Wakelin. And the play all took place in the garden of the Wakelin home. And the family were all there — and the people came and went and the story unfolded and, to some degree, the play succeeded. On the

other hand . . . the character inside my head, to whom I had been listening: the character of Cassandra Wakelin was unhappy with the way I'd handled her story. It was as if I had not provided the means by which she could tell it all. . . . I hit on the idea that Cassandra's story somehow needed to unfold *backwards*. Well . . . in the original version, Cass ends up in an insane asylum: driven there by her perception of the real world being a madhouse. . . . But — what if I were to *begin* the play in the asylum? What if I were to show the "madhouse" as the world? Then the perceptions of Cassandra Wakelin would be crystal clear to everyone. Her view of the world would fall into place for the rest of us, and her story could unfold in a way that made it easier for her to tell and for us to receive.

*Can You See Me Yet?* is a difficult and disturbing play. One of the few voices to praise it was that of novelist Margaret Laurence, who predicted that it would be performed for many years to come. It has, however, rarely been staged. Critic John F. Hulcoop sees the fact that it has been less frequently performed than other Canadian plays to be consistent with the generally poor reception of Findley's work in the 1970s. He calls the play "the most disturbing, moving, and revealing of all his fictions" before *The Wars*. Most reviews, however, were highly critical, and Findley returned to Stone Orchard vowing he would never write another play.

Dark times were never far away, and Findley's discouragement over the reception of *Can You See Me Yet?* triggered another turbulent period. For two years in the mid-1970s Bill's work took him to Ottawa; alone at Stone Orchard, Findley wrote and drank. Sometimes the drinking produced the "D.T.'s," or delirium tremens. Findley told me the story of one such episode — with a comic twist:

This time produced some monumental binges — for which, on one occasion, Bill drove back to the farm and man-handled me into the car to take me to Ottawa to sober up.

He had a large, old apartment on Cooper Street. It was at the height of a hot summer, and after Bill got me settled in one of the bedrooms, he fell asleep in one of the others — only to be awakened by my screams, coming from the living room. He bleared his way down the twisting corridor that linked the rooms of the sprawling apartment, to discover me stark naked, clutching a cushion to my mid-section, still screaming. (Bill, too, had given in to the heat and was naked.) What had happened was that a *large* bat had come down the chimney and through the fireplace. I had been awakened by this huge, soot-black figure hovering menacingly over my bed. Bill, an ex-biologist, calmly picked up a wastepaper basket, caught the animal — now thoroughly terrified — and, covering the basket with a cushion, went to put his bathrobe on before taking bat and basket outside. Bill, the bat — and I — all survived the experience.

Since this occurrence, Findley told me, he has never again experienced the D.T.'s.

Throughout even the darkest periods, Findley continued to write. Early drafts of two novels, "Desperados" and "Whisper" — "dark, depressed, and depressing; unpublished and unpublishable," in Findley's words — are among the Timothy Findley Papers in the National Archives. From "Desperados" came the title story of *Dinner Along the Amazon* and seeds of *Headhunter*. Fabiana Holback, Olivia, and early versions of Lilah Kemp and Amy Wylie are all present. As well, Findley wrote another novel during this period, one that would establish him as a major Canadian writer: *The Wars*.

## THE WARS: ORIGINS

Findley's stint as playwright-in-residence at the National Arts Centre had an even more important outcome than *Can You See Me Yet?* Something happened one night in his Ottawa room, an event that altered the course of his life: Robert Ross arrived and tapped him on the shoulder. Findley told Graeme Gibson that a work of fiction begins for him when a character, often unbidden, enters his life:

> What happens when I write? The first thing I see is the person, and the person will come and you'll hear this in your mind. (*knocking sound*); and you go to the door and you open the door and standing there is Hooker Winslow with a cat in his arms. And he says: I'm in trouble, babble, babble, babble, and a scene evolves, but it's all around the arrival of this person. It's the arrival of a person that comes first, then the milieu; where do you belong, who are your people? Then the story comes.

The story comes and Findley follows his characters' lead. He described the process to T.J. Collins:

> "You have to understand where these people walk into the story and what role they play. You have to keep control of that. But when I'm writing, people appear and disappear when they should; they come and go according to their desire to take part in the story-telling process. I often wonder why a character will come into my mind and appear in a scene, and I don't get the answer to that until three or four months later, when I suddenly discover — ah! . . . I'm impelled in the best sense of impelled — with intelligence, rather than mere obedience — not to mould, not to force, not to try to direct the traffic, but to let the traffic direct itself."

But, Findley agrees, you can't let them run wild: " 'There is a limit as to what will fit.' " Nor can the writer force a character to become his mouthpiece if the writer's views are not integral to that character:

> "Characters won't bend in directions that characters cannot go. You want them to do things because you perceive that

within the story you get a chance to tell something you want to say, but if they won't say it, you can't make them say it. You can put the words in their mouths, but it doesn't ring true and the reader knows that right off the bat."

When the character Robert Ross arrived on Findley's doorstep and tapped him on the shoulder, he was wearing a World War I uniform and riding a horse. Findley knew immediately when and where the story would take place, but not what would happen, only that the young soldier would be plunged into the horrors of war. He wrote furiously for three months as the story emerged. *The Wars* was the result, and with its publication Findley finally received critical recognition and a measure of success.

The novel is the story of Robert Ross's early adulthood. Born to a wealthy Rosedale family, Ross feels responsible when his beloved invalid sister dies. The trauma of her death impels him to leave home and join the Canadian Field Artillery. In France he endures the horrors of trench warfare, is wounded, and, upon returning to the front, commits an act that is at once treason and a life-affirming deed of heroism and love: Ross disobeys an officer, shoots him, then steals — in an effort to rescue from certain death — one hundred and thirty horses. Holed up in a barn, like Hooker Winslow in *The Last of the Crazy People*, Ross refuses to surrender as the barn is set on fire.

While working on the novel, Findley decided to spend a day and a night outdoors in November, in conditions similar to those he was describing in *The Wars*. He records the experience in his memoirs:

I went down yesterday to the foot of the lane where the fence gives way to the lower fields. There was a good deal of puddling there and everywhere the cattle have walked, they have churned up the earth, creating a kind of stew made of stones and clods of weed and mud. In the lane, I had already lost a boot and fallen on my knees so that now my trousers were soaked and one of my socks was sodden and the bottoms of both my sleeves were freezing against my wrist. . . .

I stayed there long enough to do the following . . .

— shaved in cold water

— I tried (and failed) to light a fire for boiling water

— I ate cold beans from a tin

— I emptied my bowels, using newsprint for my toilet paper. . . .

I lay down on the tarp I'd brought as a groundsheet — and tried to sleep in my sleeping bag. This was utterly impossible.

As impossible, he found, as staying out the full twenty-four hours. " 'There are so many things we cannot know unless we explore them,' " he explained to Dennis McCloskey. " 'How do you know what's under a rock unless you look?' " Findley would look under many rocks in the course of his writing life, trying to experience the details and sensations of his characters' lives.

## "AN EXTRAORDINARY CHRONICLE"

Findley read extensively while writing *The Wars* — World War I poetry, biography, memoirs, and novels — in order to portray the historical period with accuracy and provide details of trench warfare. His most important reading material was his Uncle Tif's letters from France, what Findley calls an "extraordinary chronicle" of the young soldier's war. The nineteen-year-old artillery lieutenant spent two years in the trenches before joining the Royal Flying Corps. When his plane was shot down — the pilot killed and Tif severely wounded — he was awarded the Military Cross. Young Tiff, taken to visit his dying uncle in the high white bed, was taught to revere the family's war hero, a great man as respected as grandfather Thomas Findley.

Lieutenant Tif Findley wrote to his family every day, setting down details of military training, front-line skirmishes, and life in the stinking, muddy trenches. His mother saved all of his letters, which were later typed by the secretaries at Massey-Harris and bound in a leather album. As godson, Findley was given a copy, which, when he started writing *The Wars*, provided a gold mine of research material. He used the dates and troop movements documented in the letters, as well as information garnered from Uncle Tif's descriptions of life in the trenches, all familiar to readers of *The Wars*:

April 1, 1916: The light was almost perfect from the O.P. yesterday and I saw some very interesting sights behind the German lines. A whole company of Huns drilling, an exercise ride of 16 horses and dozens of individuals were plainly visible, far beyond our range, of course.

April 3, 1916: I passed one German in our trenches that has lain wounded for four days, out in a crater in "No-man's-land," with nothing to eat. He was the most forlorn-looking spectacle I've ever seen. . . . There are no dug-outs for the men, and we passed dozens asleep on the "fire-step" of the trench, or leaning up against it.

April 19, 1916: Three large dug-outs in three days is pretty good work, and two of them are peaches. We can easily stand up in ours, and our two batmen have constructed two beds, a table and a shelf for us; besides, some of the men pinched a "has-been" stained-glass door from one of the houses in the ruined village. . . .

This last passage is clearly the basis for the stained-glass window in Robert Ross's dugout, so vividly described that it is one of *The Wars*'s most memorable images. Yet although many of the novel's vivid details are from Uncle Tif's letters, Tif was nothing like Robert Ross. Ross comes straight from Findley's fertile imagination.

Findley studied family photographs from the period too, photographs carefully saved by his grandmother and Aunt Margaret — Uncle Tif, the family car, the house on Admiral Road, a trip abroad, an iceberg. He remembers the many photographs in albums and boxes in his childhood homes, old family photos from early in the century. Many of these now reside at Stone Orchard and are brought out to show curious visitors. Findley explained his fascination with photographs in an interview with Johan Aitken:

Photographs are mysterious to me. I know it's childish, but then you have to be a child, in a way . . . in order to see at all. I still sit with a photograph and I think, if I could only get in there with you, I could walk in there, and that person is saying something, that moment in there, and one never, never, never dies.

One particular photograph that Findley saw in a newspaper has a special place in *The Wars*, a photograph of T.E. Lawrence taken during World War I. Something about the figure's bleakness, the way Lawrence's hand hangs limply at his side, attracted Findley, and it became the final image of the novel. The photograph Findley describes in the last paragraph of *The Wars* depicts Robert Ross in boot camp, sitting on a keg, a small animal skull in his hand, in a posture very similar to Lawrence's.

As well as providing research material, letters and photographs are important structural devices in *The Wars*. The novel is constructed around the voice of a narrator, an unnamed researcher, who works from letters, photographs, interviews, and clippings, to piece together Robert Ross's life. The reader is drawn into the process and becomes, in effect, the researcher. In the Aitken interview, Findley describes the shape of the novel and explains how this process works:

[W]hat I have done is make an avenue, and the avenue stretches right back to the beginning of time, and it is set up . . . of, let us say, billboards on an angle on either side of this avenue. Flashing on these billboards are the selected photographs, the images, that I wanted to imprint of moments from that war, moments from Robert's life, moments from history. . . . And then Robert . . . rides on his horse at you, down this avenue of billboards and the book keeps talking about you . . . the reader, and as you search for Robert . . . you find a little of him here, a little of him there.

## THE WARS: PUBLICATION

The story of *The Wars*'s publication is quite different from that of Findley's earlier novels. John Pearce had recently arrived from England and, as a new editor at Clarke, Irwin, he had the opportunity to search for up-and-coming writers. He wrote to the CBC Drama Department since they employed many writers. His letter was posted on a bulletin board where Stanley Colbert saw it, phoned Pearce, and suggested Timothy Findley, calling him one of the ten best writers in Canada. Pearce read *The Butterfly Plague* at Colbert's suggestion and was "bowled over, particularly by the force of the imagery." Pearce described to me his first nervous phone call to Findley:

> I phoned him about 2:15 in the afternoon and said I loved *The Butterfly Plague* and understood from Stan Colbert that he was writing a new novel about World War I. He talked about it, intriguingly, for ten or fifteen minutes and then said, "Will you excuse me a moment, I just need to make a cup of tea. When you phoned, I was writing. I've been writing all through the night and all day."

Pearce became *The Wars*'s editor, quickly recognizing that it would be the "most extraordinary" novel to be published in Canada that year. He recalls that the manuscript was "surprisingly finished" when he read it; he did relatively little editing. One suggestion he did make concerned the book's ending. Pearce told me that the evolution of *The Wars*'s conclusion was the most remarkable story he could tell me about his work with Timothy Findley:

> I felt the ending came too fast; shortly after the sequence in the barn the book just ended. "This is too abrupt," I said. "We need some time to take stock of these horrific events. We need the effect of a Greek tragedy, where the chorus leads us out to reflect." I said that one day . . . and that very night he wrote the "not yet" scene in the hospital. . . . A perfect scene written simply on the suggestion that "something" was needed. I was stunned. The scene did exactly what I had been hoping for, leading us away from those horrific events in order to reflect on them.

## SUCCESS

*The Wars* was published in 1977 by Clarke, Irwin — the first of Findley's novels to be published in Canada. It became an immediate success. Reviewer Peter Martin called it "one of the most powerful, best-crafted . . . stories it has ever been my uncomfortable pleasure to read." Myron Galloway placed it "among the finest novels to be published in this country in the past couple of decades," while Thomas R. Edwards called it "elegantly written and structured." Douglas Hill heralded Findley as "a mature and controlled artist at the peak of his remarkable powers." Such glowing reviews were a far cry from the reception of his earlier novels. To cap its critical success, *The Wars* won the 1977 Governor General's Award.

Findley came of age as a writer at an ideal time. Canadian literature was being rediscovered and reevaluated as part of an increased national pride in Canadian culture. As well, a new generation of writers was emerging. Margaret Atwood, Mordecai Richler, Margaret Laurence, Alice Munro, Robertson Davies, and Marian Engel were producing some of their best work. In the early 1970s, Findley helped found the Writers' Union

FIGURE 12

This photo of Findley, with a machine gun and memorial wreaths, was taken in Hart House Memorial Tower in Toronto. It was widely used to publicize The Wars.

of Canada, established to promote Canadian writers' interests and foster a spirit of professionalism. It was at one of the Union's early planning meetings that he first met Marian Engel, who was to become one of his closest friends.

*The Wars* was widely read, analyzed, and written about. The academic journal *Canadian Literature* devoted its 1981 winter issue to a discussion of the novel. Scholars explored such topics as the place of *The Wars* in the genres of war writing and historical fiction, the novel's themes and images, Findley's use of romantic mythical forms, and Robert Ross as a tragic hero. In other articles, critics focused on the violence in the novel, or examined Findley's use of photographs and other postmodern devices. *The Wars* continues to be studied in high-school and university courses and has been translated into many languages.

With the success of *The Wars*, Findley gained some measure of fame and financial security. He became recognized as a leading writer and was asked to serve as chairman of the Writers' Union in 1977, and as the University of Toronto's writer-in-residence the following year. He won the Toronto Book Award and was named Author of the Year by the Periodical Distributors of Canada. Friendships with other writers encouraged and sustained him. There were many late-night phone conversations with Margaret Laurence, Phyllis Webb, and Marian Engel — in a variety of states of sobriety and intoxication, Findley adds — fellow writers who understood the joys and agonies of writing. Many writers praised his work in articles and reviews. When *The Wars* came out, he was particularly heartened by Margaret Atwood's incisive review in the *Financial Post*. For the first time he felt his work was being understood and appreciated.

## ANOTHER PLAY

Writing for the theatre still held a strong attraction for Findley, so despite his disappointment with *Can You See Me Yet?*, he agreed to write for the stage again, returning to the historical period of

*The National Dream* and to its star, William Hutt. At the time, Hutt was artistic director at Theatre London and commissioned his old friend and colleague to write a play for the 1978–79 season. Hutt would once again play Canada's first prime minister in the première production of *John A. — Himself!*

Director Peter Moss explained to Doug Bale that Findley based the play on the premise that actors and politicians are of a similar type. As Findley's Macdonald looks back on his political career, he sees it as a dramatic performance: " 'The John A. Macdonald Show — Twenty-four years in Her Majesty's Theatre, Ottawa!' " The first act is modelled on Victorian music-hall entertainment, popular in Macdonald's time. With an assortment of highly coloured theatrics — including ventriloquism, magic, and a circus act in which Louis Riel appears as Louis La Mouche, The Human Fly — Findley reveals the man behind the actor/politician mask.

In the second act, Victorian comedy gives way to Victorian pathos as the conventions of melodrama take over. Findley chose a vaudeville approach because he wanted to make the play more *"theatrical."* He told *London Free Press* critic Bale that he believed the theatre's "essential reason for being" is its theatricality, something he felt many present-day playwrights had lost sight of.

Reviews of *John A. — Himself!* were cautiously favourable. Audrey Ashley credited Findley and Hutt with creating a "living portrait" of Canada's first prime minister but thought the conflicting styles and approaches resulted in a "disconcerting" experience for the audience. In his review, Bale suggested that the play was much like Canadian history: "moments of inspired achievement alternating with periods of humdrum and triviality."

## FAMOUS LAST WORDS

Encouraged by the continued success of *The Wars*, Findley began another novel — also involving a world war — but this time a more ambitious work, broader in scope and ideas, more complex in style. For many years he had been intrigued by the Duke and Duchess of Windsor, by glimpses of their decadent lives and hints of their fascist sympathies before and during World War II. The Duchess had actually entered his life, as Mrs. Simpson, when he was just a child. Findley told the story as his contribution to "True Tales of Toronto":

There was a famous figure . . . whose fame, around the time I was 6, became rather alarmingly personal to me. This was the woman who came and cleaned our house every Tuesday and Friday. I have never known a woman so dour and endlessly unhappy. She never smiled and was given to heaving sighs halfway up the stairs. This woman, whose name was Mrs. Simpson, was tall and extremely thin . . . and wore her hair very tightly bound underneath a net. Her skin tone was grey. One day in December of 1936, the lady in question was standing on the landing leaning on her broom and heaving one of her sighs when the paper arrived. My mother unfolded it — as she did on any other day — and suddenly cried out: "My God! *The King is going to marry Mrs. Simpson!*" To me, of course, there was only one Mrs. Simpson and she lived in Toronto. But . . . why would the King want to marry *her*?

His fascination with the former Mrs. Simpson and her ex-king, combined with hundreds of hours of reading about the people and events that surrounded them, gave Findley the germ of his new novel. He used many historical figures as well as scores of invented characters, combining historical fact with imaginative fiction.

Unlike *The Wars*, there was no early moment of recognition with *Famous Last Words*, no fully formed character tapping him on the shoulder. Consequently, the novel went through many drafts in the four years it took to write. Findley sometimes felt that the story had been "given to the wrong person." He recalls that he nearly wore out the floor between his room and Bill's as he planned and rejected and agonized over each successive draft. "I can't do it," he would despair, and then go back and try once more. However unfit he felt, the story had been given to him; he had to get it down on paper.

John Pearce read through several drafts of the emerging novel, never despairing of its eventual completion because he recognized that its "core" was always there. One day he suggested to Findley that the book needed a central character or event to pull together its disparate threads. As Pearce told me, "Tiff took that suggestion away and I waited to see what might happen. What happened was that one night he was reading Ezra Pound and came across the Hugh Selwyn Mauberley poem and . . . essentially said 'Ah ha.'"

With that "Ah ha," Findley found his central character as well as the form his story would take. "When I first saw Mauberley," Findley explained to Terry Goldie, "I had a flash vision of him standing on a chair, wearing a great coat. . . . putting images on the walls and ceilings." The tap on the shoulder was a little slow in coming, perhaps, but when Findley finally discovered his pivotal character in Pound's poem, the novel began to take shape. Mauberley became the voice of the novel; his words became the "famous last words."

The novel's plots and characters became so complex that at one point Findley constructed a large display board for his dozens of characters, arranging them in various configurations. Only a few of the original number made it to the final draft. One of Findley's favourite characters, Jane Porter, was cut from the novel on the advice of editor John Pearce. Findley reluctantly agreed with Pearce's argument that Mauberley, knowing he had little time to live, would only record the main elements of his story, but he found it painful to cut Jane Porter. A few years later he published the excerpt in *Inside Memory*.

When the novel was finished it covered an extensive span of European history and was peopled with over twenty fictional characters and fifty historical figures, including the Windsors, Rudolph Hess, Ezra Pound, Sir Harry Oakes, and Lana Turner.

Mauberley, a writer who becomes involved in the intrigue of a fascist cabal surrounding the Windsors, narrates the complex story, etching it on the walls of the Grand Elysium Hotel in the Austrian Alps before he is murdered. In telling his story, he also records the facts that will condemn him as a fascist sympathizer.

In a double framing device, American Lieutenant Quinn, given the task of decoding the writing on the walls after Mauberley's body is found, reads Mauberley's "famous last words" with sympathy; his superior, Captain Freyberg, assesses them with contempt. As in *The Wars*, the reader is drawn into the task of deciphering the slippery truth of Mauberley's story, as well as that of conventional historical accounts of the period. Adding another layer of complexity, Mauberley's story begins, *"All I have written here . . . is true; except the lies."*

*Famous Last Words* is Findley's most extensive study of fascism, a theme that runs insistently throughout his work. The novel poses a question. Mauberley, who gains the reader's sympathies, becomes involved with fascists — What is it about fascism that attracts him? *The Butterfly Plague* suggests one answer: fascism seems to offer the promise of perfection. *Famous Last Words* postulates that we are seduced by the power and glamour of the élite. Findley believes that the "seeds of fascism" lie dormant within us all and that the realization of this fact is our best defence against it. " 'Mauberley is in everyone,' " he told Bruce Blackadar, " 'we're all fascists. . . . Whenever we can't accomplish anything, we use force to get what we want. . . . I wanted to find out why people like Mauberley needed to be so repressive. Fascism is a neurotic refusal to face reality.' "

Findley went on to describe how vividly he remembers the atmosphere of the war years:

"I grew up in that period, and it clings to the hem of my memory. I was a watcher as a kid, and I never forgot how it all looked, and smelled. It was like overhearing the build-up of the traumatic horrors that were coming."

Young Tiff listened to war speeches, heard Hitler on the radio, and watched newsreels at the cinema on the wars in China and Spain. Images of the fascist regimes in Europe came to him night after night — in epic scale.

*Famous Last Words* was enthusiastically received and extensively reviewed in Canada and the United States. *New York Times* reviewer Christopher Lehmann-Haupt called it a "remarkable new novel," while Canadian reviews heralded the invention of Mauberley as narrator a stroke of genius, Nancy A. Schiefer christening the novel a "major event of the Canadian book season." Although reviewers and readers admired the technical virtuosity of the book, many found it a difficult work. Paul Roberts summed it up as "excessive, and mad, and marvellous, puzzling, disturbing and utterly brilliant." The novel that took four years to write, that caused Findley to wonder if it had been given to the wrong writer, was another success for the now respected, and celebrated, novelist. Timothy Findley had gained the stature of a major Canadian writer.

Yet because of prohibitive European libel laws, Findley was advised not to publish *Famous Last Words* in Britain and France while the Duchess of Windsor was still alive. At the time, the Duchess was in her eighties, ill, and living in seclusion in Paris. One evening in 1985, as he and Bill Whitehead (whom Findley often refers to as WFW) watched the CBC Television news, Knowlton Nash reached the end of the broadcast when obituaries of famous people are usually read. Findley tells the story in his memoirs:

> He gave a small, slightly sad smile and his voice dropped just a bit in volume as he said: *and finally, tonight in Paris, the Duchess of Windsor quietly . . .*
>
> WFW and I both automatically leaned forward, the word already echoing in our minds: *died* — along with the relief that at last the book could be published in Britain and France! The thought of movie sales, mass-market paperbacks and Johnny Carson danced around the ceiling.

And then, as smoothly as ever, Knowlton completed his announcement.

*. . . celebrated her eighty-ninth birthday.*

After a stunned moment, WFW and I looked at each other — more in shame than anything else, and then, without saying a word, we raised our glasses, with their last few sips of wine, and offered silent tribute to a remarkable — if maddening — woman.

In 1987 *Famous Last Words* was finally published in Britain to scathing reviews, most of them predictably focusing on Findley's irreverent portrayal of the Windsors. Although the reviews were personally devastating to Findley, they did not impede sales of the book. In fact, they had the opposite effect, and the novel became an overnight best seller. After a harrowing book-signing tour in England, Findley and Whitehead quietly crossed the channel for a holiday in Dieppe.

## *THE WARS* ON FILM

With publication in Britain and France and translation into several languages, *Famous Last Words* consolidated Findley's international reputation and generated renewed interest in his earlier novels. In 1983 Penguin Books reissued *The Last of the Crazy People* in paperback; that same year *The Wars* was made into a film.

Findley's experience as screenwriter for this film was more rewarding than his previous film work, perhaps because his writing was by now more respected, perhaps because he was working with an extremely talented group of artists. Stratford veteran Robin Phillips directed the production. Findley admired Phillips's approach to the film, particularly his ability to convey subtle meaning through gesture and his openness to the creative inspiration of a chance event. An episode from the filmset confirms Findley's impression. Findley described to Terry Goldie the filming of the hospital scene in which Robert Ross first meets Lady Barbara D'Orsey:

> Then she walks on and you know that she's going to have to come to Robert. She disappears behind a screen and then steps out the other side. When she does this, she stops and she looks around *everywhere but at Robert*, and Robert is glued to her. Then the chance thing happens that Robin Phillips is brilliant at catching. As Barbara steps back, out of sight, *the floor creaks*, and that sound is like something yawning open underneath the whole building — and, indeed, the whole safe world. This is the first indication of what Barbara represents. Then she's gone. But it so happens it was just happenstance that the floor creaked! Another director might have cursed and asked them to fix the floor-boards and re-shot the scene. But Phillips was open to the suggestion the sound gave him and he used it.

They worked with some of the country's most respected stage actors, including Brent Carver, William Hutt, Jackie Burroughs, and Martha Henry. Henry, now artistic director of London's Grand Theatre, played the part of Mrs. Ross and recalls working with Findley on the set:

> He was constantly here and there, never interfering, but always available and always curious, excited and supportive. He told a number of stories during those days of filming, none of which I remember now (they all had to do with feeding me information about the Mrs. Rosses of his life) but all of which moved me a little further toward the richness of that remarkable character. . . . It's a tribute to Tiff that he is able to feed his knowledge into the oblivion that becomes the food for a character's creative background, rather than being the storyteller who brings the focus back upon himself. Tiff is one of the few people I know who is ego-less when it comes to his creations. . . . As a result, in a

filming situation one is only aware of his generosity; he gives everything away.

William Hutt, relating his experience of working with Findley in dramatic productions over the course of many years, echoes Henry's comments: "He never threw his ego on the line, never said this is what I want and we're going to have it. Suggestions were made and Tiff was very amenable but never subservient. . . . He compromised if he felt that that was the right thing for the play. He is one of the most radiantly humble people I know."

Despite the pleasure of working with Robin Phillips and the distinguished cast, there were disappointments in filming *The Wars*. An inadequate budget prevented filming many of the scenes that would have given the film the panoramic scope of the novel, and working with the National Film Board, the co-producer, was an exercise in frustration. Some of those involved in the production didn't even seem to understand the novel. Findley gave me a classic example of this lack of understanding: an NFB executive who said, "If this is called '*The Wars*,' why are we spending all this time with that family in Toronto?"

The music for the film was composed by well-known pianist and composer, Glenn Gould. Gould created the score using music that was indigenous to the story's time and place, music that might be found in the piano bench in the Ross's Rosedale drawing room. When Gould died at the age of fifty, shortly after completing his music for *The Wars*, Findley gathered with friends and colleagues at Toronto's St. Paul's Church for a memorial service. In a review of a biography of Gould, Findley recalled that Gould's favourite scene in the film was the one shot at St. Paul's. He described the service:

As we sat in the crowded church, there seemed to be a lot of silence. There wasn't, of course. People spoke. We shouted hymns. Maureen Forrester stood somewhere to my right and sang "Have Mercy, Lord" from the St Matthew Passion. Then, I think, the silence I remember did in fact descend, and out of that silence everyone sitting — hundreds of us, each one sitting alone — heard the first painfully haunting notes of the *Aria da capo*. . . .

During the 1980s Findley attended more memorial services, as several friends and colleagues died relatively young: Marian Engel in 1985, Margaret Laurence and poet Gwendolyn MacEwen in 1987, and critic Ken Adachi in 1989. Findley wrote tributes for them all, recalling amusing moments from the times their lives had overlapped with his, and sat in the silence of memorial services similar to that for Glenn Gould. At such moments he recalled a favourite line of the musician: " 'To exist for a while is better than never to exist at all.' "

### SAINT FRANCIS OF CANNINGTON

When he was first approached about writing the music for the film version of *The Wars*, Glenn Gould read the novel. He said he loved the story and wanted to do the music, but was horrified at the thought of filming scenes that involved cruelty to animals. Gould stipulated that he would work on the film only if he were assured that no animals would be injured or killed during filming. The guarantee was given and the contract signed. A veterinarian was present throughout the filming, and all of the scenes involving animal death and injury were simulated.

Gould's position was one with which Findley was in full sympathy. Findley's love and respect for animals is reflected in his writing and his life. Visitors to Stone Orchard never fail to comment on the collection of twenty-some cats gathered on the sunny veranda. Over the years, the farmstead has also been home to horses rescued from the glue factory — including Findley's favourite, Bill-the-Horse — and to several dogs. Bill Whitehead affectionately calls his companion Saint Francis of Cannington because he has given refuge to so many animals.

FIGURE 13

*Findley and one of the many residents at Stone Orchard, Bill-the-Horse. "A great-hearted animal," he wrote to me. "I got lucky when he came along."*

Creatures from the woods and fields also share Stone Orchard with the human inhabitants. Birds flock to the many feeders. A large family of raccoons makes a nightly raid on the catfood dishes on the veranda, creating an unholy racket. Bill Whitehead told Veronica Cusack the story of Ingrid the mouse:

"There was a mouse with a withered eye who used to come up onto the kitchen counter to see what crumbs were available. We could recognize her, and we called her Ingrid. She somehow could get into the dishwasher. I never understood that — if the water couldn't get out, I don't know how she could get in. But we had to check it every time, because we came to love her. We are in a fairly evangelical part of the country and one day — I was getting a meal ready and dealing with the phone that wouldn't shut up — there was a knock on the door. I peered around the window and there was the familiar sight of a pale face and pamphlets. I slammed the dishwasher shut, turned it on, dashed to the door, and my first words were, 'Oh, Christ; I forgot about Ingrid.' I dashed back into the kitchen and found the terrified creature cowering among the jets of water. 'Darling, I'm so sorry,' I said, and then called out 'I'll be right with you; I'm just drying the mouse.' When I got back, they'd gone."

Findley's belief in preserving the natural world has also led him to fight for environmental causes. Recently neighbours have been meeting at Stone Orchard to plan a campaign to save the Beaver River wetlands. Similarly, several years ago, in an effort to stop trapping in the area, Findley bought the local hardware store's entire supply of leg-hold traps. When the stock was replenished, he bought those too, but soon realized his efforts were futile. The supply of traps appeared to be infinite, his funds were not.

Findley has many stories about how he acquired and named the animals that have shared his life. The cat Gigi was born at the precise moment Findley learned that *The Wars* had won the

Governor General's Award. Findley told me the story of the early-morning birth:

> The great Gigi, our thirteen-year companion, was born in the room where Bill was working. We'd been up half the night with the mother who was having a very difficult birth. She had had four kittens and Gigi was the fifth and the last. I was taking a bath and the phone rang just as he was being born and the mother cried out in pain. I got out and sat all wrapped up in towels, soaking wet, and the person on the other end said, "How do you do, my name is so-and-so," in this very French-Canadian accent. "I am delighted to tell you *The Wars* has won the Governor General's Award." So we called the kitten G.G. for Governor General and then, because he was so elegant, he became Gigi.

## "OBSESSIONS": *DINNER ALONG THE AMAZON*

Findley had been writing short stories ever since Ruth Gordon's challenge inspired his youthful "About Effie" in the early 1950s. Several were published in the 1970s, three of them in *Tamarack Review*, and others were read on CBC Radio's *Anthology*. In 1984, Penguin published Findley's first collection of short fiction, *Dinner Along the Amazon*. It included all of these stories plus the title piece, a new story set in Rosedale that explores the complexities of human relationships. *Dinner Along the Amazon* thus traces Findley's development as a short-story writer over the thirty years since he first wrote to show Ruth Gordon that young people did have something positive to say.

In his introduction to the collection, Findley describes its themes and images as his "personal obsessions":

> It came as something of a shock, when gathering these stories for collective publication, to discover that for over

thirty years of writing my attention has turned again and again to the same unvarying gamut of sounds and images. They not only turn up here in this present book, but in my novels, too. I wish I hadn't noticed this. In fact, it became an embarrassment and I began to wonder if I should file A CATALOGUE OF PERSONAL OBSESSIONS. The sound of screen doors banging; evening lamplight; music held at a distance — always being played on a gramophone; letters written on blue-tinted note paper; robins making forays onto summer lawns to murder worms; photographs in cardboard boxes; Colt revolvers hidden in bureau drawers and a chair that is always falling over. What does it mean? Does it mean that here is a writer who is hopelessly uninventive? Appallingly repetitive? Why are the roads always dusty in this man's work — why is it always so *hot* — why can't it RAIN? And my agent was once heard to moan aloud as she was reading through the pages of a television script I had just delivered: "Oh God, Findley — *not more rabbits!*"

Reviewers also noted Findley's self-described obsessions, highlighting the consistent themes of loneliness and longing, betrayal, guilt, and regret that permeate the stories. They identified a particular character type, dubbed "Findley's people." According to Alberto Manguel, "Findley's people. . . . are always occupied, a group obsessed with collecting whatever evidence about themselves is available . . . trying to understand their world." Findley's method, Manguel writes, is to establish an acceptable, ordinary world, and people it "with characters who fail to understand it." The reader must then join the characters in investigating their dilemma. Other critics praised Findley's craftsmanship and technical brilliance but approached his characters coolly, calling them depressing or mad. The world of Findley's people was summed up by H.R. Percy as "a great place to visit but you wouldn't want to live there."

FIGURE 14

*Mottle, the blind cat who inspired* Not Wanted on the Voyage, *with Bill Whitehead.*

The beginnings of Findley's next novel go back to a fall day in 1970 when he found on the road near Stone Orchard a starving, blind cat whom he adopted and named Mottle. She lived with him for several years, one of the few cats not relegated to porch and barn, but given full access to the house. Findley admired her courage and resourcefulness and felt a special bond with Mottle, who, he thought, related to him not just as a caregiver, but as a fellow creature. When she died in 1981, he started writing a novel with Mottle as a character. He changed the spelling of her name to Mottyl, put her in turn-of-the-century rural Ontario, and gave her as mistress a downtrodden, gin-loving farm wife who thumped out hymns on the piano. There was a blizzard in the story and into it the woman's abusive husband disappears.

This was the original setting, but something was wrong, the novel was not working — until a chance event changed the direction of the remarkable novel that would become *Not Wanted on the Voyage*.

Poet Phyllis Webb, a long-time friend of Findley, had come from her home on Saltspring Island in British Columbia to attend a feminist conference in Toronto, and Findley went to hear her read some of her new poems. One of them was called "Leaning." In it, Webb uses the image of the Leaning Tower of Pisa with all of humankind's artists and scientists crammed inside. In slow motion the tower begins to fall — it will either crash to the earth or launch into space. The poem concludes: "And you, are you still here / tilting in this stranded ark / blind and seeing in the dark." In his memoirs, Findley describes his reaction to the poem:

Hearing these words — I made a sort of strangled sound — like *oomph!* It was just as if I had been struck in the solar plexus.

In that moment, the whole of *Not Wanted on the Voyage* fell into place. *All* of it.

Why?

Because, in her poem, Phyllis Webb had used the words *ark* and *blind* and *dark* — and all at once, I knew who all my people were and what their predicament was. The gin-loving farm wife was Mrs Noyes — the abusive farmer was her husband, Noah — the blizzard was the Great Flood and Mrs Noyes would not get on the Ark without her cat — the blind cat, Mottyl. . . .

On this new course, the writing went more smoothly, but once again Findley wanted to experience firsthand the events he was writing about. For *The Wars* this involved a day spent outdoors in mud and freezing rain; for *Not Wanted on the Voyage* it entailed imagining how a blind cat would "see" the world. One of the stories Findley often tells at readings is how he was discovered early one morning on a Tofino beach, crawling along on all fours, eyes closed, "my bum in the air and nose in the sand," by a couple who, thinking he was on drugs, warned their children away and debated calling "the authorities." "It certainly is a lesson, George, of what addiction does to a person," concluded the woman. The addiction was, after all, quite harmless: simply the writer trying to experience his character's view of the world.

In the simplest of terms, *Not Wanted on the Voyage* is an imaginative retelling of the Genesis story of Noah and the Ark. Like *The Wars* and *Famous Last Words*, the novel blends biblical "fact" with inventive fiction. Noah is transformed into Dr. Noyes, a sadistic and lecherous tyrant; God is Yaweh, a tottering old man with food in his beard who opts for his own death; and Lucifer appears as Lucy, a kindly seven-foot angel in drag. There are sheep that sing hymns, unicorns, faeries, and, of course, Mrs. Noyes, and Mottyl, the cat.

The novel's title refers to the labels put on steamer trunks not needed during an ocean voyage. On this voyage, as in the Bible, only Noah's family and a chosen pair of each animal species are wanted. Old and blind, Mottyl is among the "not wanted," but Mrs. Noyes smuggles her aboard. The pair represents a universal life force; Mottyl gives birth and Mrs. Noyes prays to "an absent

FIGURE 15

*Findley and Ezra at "Arkwright," the farmhouse across the road where most of* Not Wanted on the Voyage *was written.*

cloud" for more rain. Somehow Mrs. Noyes and the others on the ark work out a fragile system of support, though she dreads what will happen if Noah has the opportunity to start a new world.

Findley points out that the landscape of *Not Wanted on the Voyage* is not an exotic, long-ago biblical place but is firmly rooted in southern Ontario. Noah's hill is just beyond the field; his ark is the big blue barn across the road from Stone Orchard. Much of the novel was written in the farmhouse beside that barn, where Findley lived while good friend and neighbour Len Collins — Findley calls him "a kind of construction genius" — built an addition at Stone Orchard. They called the farmhouse "Arkwright," and while living there Findley spent a night with the animals in the great blue barn. He told Alan Twigg, "It became my ark. . . . I spent a whole night there just so I could listen in the dark. It's wonderful to go in the dark with all those creatures. To be in their darkness."

If the landscape is familiar, so are the novel's themes. Read as a metaphor for our times, it addresses contemporary concerns: feminism, the destruction of the environment, cruelty to animals, and the danger of fundamentalist thinking. Findley's deliberate use of anachronism forces the reader to experience the story in the present: people ride around in democrat wagons, Albert Einstein and Walt Whitman are mentioned, and Yaweh has a pair of cats named Abraham and Sarah.

Critics called *Not Wanted on the Voyage* Findley's most feminist novel. From the earliest stories, Findley's fiction has had strong female characters depicted with great sympathy. Findley consistently expresses horror at the injustices in women's lives and is outspoken about the dangers of ignoring women's oppression. As he said to Pearl Sheffy Gefen, "It's about bloody time men acknowledged that nothing good can happen in this world until they recognize that women are literally half of the human race and have been making immense contributions all along. . . . Men have always underscored the differences they see, shutting women out." Critic Lorraine York suggests that all of Findley's work expresses feminist concerns, but until he used the more explicit narrative voice of Mrs. Noyes, critics were slow to recognize it. She sees Findley's entire oeuvre as one system: "a system of warfare wherein gender, as a variable, plays an increasingly dominant role."

Findley has great affection for his women friends as well as his women characters. He told Gefen that he had "accepted the fact of his homosexuality from his earliest years," but hastened to add,

"I adore women. I was married to a woman whom I loved greatly and still do. I've loved many women, but not in the physical sense, and that was where my wife and I made our mistake. We thought we could have a marriage without that, and you can't, not if she wants children, which she did. So we parted amicably. But I could no more live in a world without women than in a world without men."

*Not Wanted on the Voyage* is dedicated to one of these women friends, Phyllis Webb, but even with the inspiration of her poem, writing the novel did not come easily to Findley. As the writing faltered, he was hounded once again by feelings of self-doubt and bouts of heavy drinking. Sometimes Findley would sit up all night in the old wicker chair in the study with a wine glass in hand, the bottle on the table, and just enough light to hit the ashtray with his cigarette ash. He made late-night phone calls to patient friends, who listened to his outpourings of frustration and despair.

At these times, Findley doubted that he could ever write again. Then he would remember Thornton Wilder's advice to leave the passage that wouldn't work and go on to something that came more easily: "Above all, don't stop writing." He told himself not to explain, not to *write* but to *tell* the story of the blind cat in the ark. Think of an audience, he told himself; think of Bill; tell Bill. Be the storyteller.

*Not Wanted on the Voyage* was published in 1984 to enthusiastic reviews. John Moss called the book "a thing of wonder, one of the truly great books . . . a deeply moving and beautifully written novel," and placed Findley at the forefront of Canadian writing. Some reviewers discussed the novel as a cautionary fable dealing with contemporary issues; others praised Findley's style and imagination. Writer and critic George Woodcock believed the novel expressed a view of the natural order and the nature of God consistent with Gnosticism, a system of religious and philosophical doctrine combining Christian beliefs with Greek and Oriental philosophy. Although Findley does not subscribe to Gnosticism or any other religious doctrine, he has often expressed his view that the sacred can be found in the natural world.

When Findley was working on the novel and realized it would be about the Great Flood of Genesis, he set about reading religious texts and commentary. He remembers discovering the theory that civilization started to fall apart when humans chose one God over a belief in the holiness of all living things. At that moment, as the theory has it, the natural world lost its sacredness. But Findley has long believed that everything that lives is sacred. In a 1973 interview with Donald Cameron, he said his motto was, "Make peace with nature, now." More recently, talking with Alan Twigg, he reflected on the significance of Mrs. Noyes praying to the river:

It seems to me that by removing ourselves from nature we're losing our imaginations. The creative way of looking at things instead of the passive or destructive way. . . . I love Mrs. Noyes praying to the river. Why not? Pray to everything that is. If God is really everywhere . . . then why not pray to God through rivers, trees and animals? God isn't somewhere out of sight. At least not my god. And not the god of Mrs. Noyes. That god exists in everything that breathes.

Surprisingly, few readers of *Not Wanted on the Voyage* complained of Findley's turning Judeo-Christian mythology on its head. Only when the novel was later made into a play did fundamentalists voice their objections.

*Not Wanted on the Voyage* was released in paperback and published in the United States in 1985. Like *The Wars* and *Famous Last Words*, it has been translated into several languages. It won the Canadian Authors Association Literary Award for best novel in 1985 and was short-listed for the Governor General's Award.

Also in 1985, Findley was asked to revise *The Butterfly Plague*. With some reluctance, he agreed, hoping to give a second chance to a novel that had been so little understood and so poorly received that he calls it his "stillborn child." In the preface to the new edition, he wrote of the original, "It was a good idea, but its time had not come. Or rather, its writer had not made sure of his craft. He simply wrote it too soon." After five novels, Findley had certainly perfected his craft, but the revised edition, as Findley told me, was as "shabbily" treated as the first. "Perhaps," he suggested, "it is too much an allegory."

Yet Findley continued to gain recognition as one of Canada's top fiction writers. His books were selling well, winning awards, and being discussed in critical journals and university courses. He was frequently interviewed about his work and asked for his opinion on issues of concern to writers. Already — in 1982 and in 1984 — he had received two honorary degrees. In 1985 he served as writer-in-residence at the University of Winnipeg, and the following year was made an Officer of the Order of Canada. Timothy Findley had come a long way from the unknown writer who could not get published in his own country.

## ON TOUR

With increased public stature and escalating book sales, the often-dreaded author's tour became a regular part of Findley's life. For six to eight weeks after publication of each novel, he and

Bill travel from one end of the country to the other, reading in schools, libraries, and community centres; signing books; and giving interviews, again and again. By the final days of the tour, Findley is usually ill with a heavy cold, but each night as he mounts yet another stage and steps up to another podium, the discipline of the theatre takes over. In his best actor's voice, with dramatic gestures and significant pauses, the reading begins, usually with an anecdote related to the work he is about to read.

Book tours, Findley writes in "Alarms and Excursions," are dreadful in prospect: "[u]prooting and disorienting, tiring and fraught with alarming confrontations" — but mandatory. If you write books, he says, it goes with the territory. He doesn't use the tours to flog his books, but rather sees them as an opportunity to make contact with readers and present his work in the best possible way. Writers should be glad their books get attention, he continues in the article:

> To be frank, I'm put off by writers whose publishers have gone to a hell of a lot of trouble and no small expense to send them across the country, and to whom the people in the various media have at least given their attention, who then return from their tours and bitch about the whole experience. A lot of books get published in a season — hundreds. And of the hundreds, maybe 20 or 30 get anything like the attention they deserve. If your book has been lucky enough to garner any part of that attention, believe me, you are very lucky.

Findley told me that people think he enjoys giving readings because he enjoyed acting, but the truth is, he didn't enjoy acting. Every performance was a nerve-wracking experience. (Of course, he adds, I wouldn't have been an actor if I hadn't wanted to be.) He explained how, early on, he figured out how to get through readings:

> I decided what I would do was play the role of the writer. I had done this once before, selling books when I was between

acting jobs. One day I had stood there in the bookstore feeling wholly inadequate, watching a woman crossing the floor who I knew was going to ask for my help. "Wait a minute," I said to myself, "this is just another acting job." I played the role of the bookseller. And, bam! I sold books by the dozens. I found the secret was this: play it as a role. So now I play the writer. Otherwise I could not get through it.

Findley has a collection of stories about reading-tour incidents: the interviewers who haven't read his book, the time he set off the fire alarm in the old Carnegie library in Calgary, and the reading during an unprecedented snowstorm in Victoria with only the town drunk and an old deaf woman in attendance. In "The Sound of Writers Reading," Findley related one experience at a small college in Kingston:

> "It was a noon hour affair. Students were pouring through the halls. I finally found the room I was to read in. The audience consisted of three students who were reluctant, to say the least. They'd obviously been made to come. . . . They sat in a cluster in one corner looking glum.
>
> "But, stage right, the rest of the audience sat. It was two other students who had clearly wandered into the wrong room and were somewhat startled when I began to read. They were eating their lunch and they did everything but pop the lunch bag. When they'd finished eating, they got up and left, halfway through my reading, which was really kind of a relief. I only had to look in one direction, at the three students who were staring stonily at me."

"And then," Findley paused dramatically as we talked about reading-tour horror stories, "there was the time that Bill tricked me":

> I was so tired. . . . We had been to Ottawa and Toronto and many other places and we got back home and Bill said, "Now we're going to Lindsay." And I said, "No, we're not." "But," Bill said, "all you have to do is read and there will be

just a few people and it's a local situation. . . ." So we went. A charming local writer had organized the evening. There were many people; they had to get more chairs, but then I turned and saw the sign. It said, "Timothy Findley will speak on the subject of. . . ." And I looked at Bill and said, "I don't understand, I thought I was going to read." "Well, if I had told you that you were to give a little talk you wouldn't have come . . . and besides, you're *so* good on your feet."

Findley survived the evening ("It actually went quite well") — just as he had in Kingston, Victoria, and Calgary — by playing the role of the writer. That trick, and having Bill with him — "the perfect combination of road manager and travelling companion" — helps him through the many arduous reading tours.

## THE ATLANTIC HOUSE HOTEL

For his next novel, *The Telling of Lies*, Findley experimented with a new genre — the murder mystery. Like some of his earlier work, the idea for it came to him in one flash, this time as he sat on the beach of the Atlantic House Hotel on the coast of Maine. Findley's family had a long tradition of summer holidays at the Atlantic House, from early in the century when his father was a small boy. The details of the four-storey, white clapboard hotel — which became the Aurora Sands Hotel in *The Telling of Lies* — with its wide green lawn and long sandy beach, are forever etched in Findley's memory. And, as Findley wrote in his memoirs, so are some of the hotel's regular guests:

When I was a teenager, I used to nervously avoid what had been dubbed *Stonehenge* — the monumental, stone-faced gathering of matriarchs who, long ago, had claimed one corner of the lobby. I remember vividly their piercing, all-seeing eyes, their thin-lipped mouths and the furs around their necks. I was absolutely convinced they had killed the animals they wore with their very own hands — or possibly by spitting venom.

Findley continued to visit the Atlantic House until it was burned down in 1986 to make way for a condominium development. The surrounding marshlands were also destroyed, making Findley furious.

Well before this event, however, one day on the Atlantic House beach, sitting off to one side, away from the main group gathered around the deck chairs and beach umbrellas, Findley began to mentally film the scene playing in his mind: this scene was to form the germ of *The Telling of Lies*. He described the process for Alberto Manguel:

> I imagined a sequence of slow dissolves in which there was no one, and then there was the first person, who would be the beach boy, and then slowly the beach fills, and then it grows and there's this huge mass of a hundred people all clustered together, jabbering and drinking gin and children screaming and all this kind of thing; and then it slowly dissolves — boom-boom-boom — and right in the centre of the final dissolve is a dead person in a deck chair, violently murdered, who has been killed in the midst of this great kafuffle of people.

## MURDER AND METHOD:
### *THE TELLING OF LIES*

While Findley realized that he was in the midst of a murder mystery, he insists now that the book is primarily a novel, a novel written within the conventions of detective fiction. These conventions created certain technical difficulties and forced him to write in a different way. With previous novels the characters had presented themselves to Findley and he had followed along to see where they would lead. Sometimes they did quite surprising things, such as Hooker's final act of murder in *The Last of the*

*Crazy People*. But with *The Telling of Lies*, Findley began with the story itself; his characters' actions were constrained by the workings of the plot.

There was, however, one "character" that did present itself to Findley, demanding to be included in the story. As he described it, he was mentally walking his narrator along the beach, when an iceberg suddenly appeared — an unlikely occurrence in midsummer off the coast of Maine. At first Findley threw down his pen, unwilling to allow it into the story, but thirty years of trusting his impulses convinced him to let it stay. He decided to make it as symbolic as possible, giving it the shape of the Capitol Building in Washington, District of Columbia. An iceberg, with most of its surface hidden under the water, is also a classic image of deceit.

Findley's detective is a memorable character called Vanessa van Horne, an ageing landscape architect and photographer, who is reluctantly drawn into the search for the murderer of a contemptible pharmaceutical magnate (the body found on the beach). Findley invents for Vanessa a remarkable childhood — she and her family spent World War II in a Japanese prison camp — that counterpoints the murder plot. She is modelled on a woman from New York named Dorothy Warren, whom Findley had known for many years as a fellow guest at the Atlantic House. When Findley asked her permission to base his character on her, Warren agreed on two conditions: that her character not be involved in any bizarre sex scenes, and that no one was to know she was the prototype. She was pleased enough with her fictional counterpart, however, to identify herself proudly. Twelve of Dorothy Warren's black-and-white photographs of the Atlantic House Hotel decorate Findley's studio, and since the hotel's destruction, she spends her summer holidays with her old friends at Stone Orchard.

The challenge of writing his novel with a female narrator — a first for Findley — was compounded by the realization that he would have to tell the story in the first person. As Findley explained to Suzanne Sandor:

Once I had made the discovery that Vanessa was the central character, I tried writing it in the third person, and that had a lot of advantages. I really wanted to write this book in the third person with Vanessa as a character observed along with a number of others. But that didn't give the sense of "closing in," and the best way to show that is to lock yourself into one voice.

Much of Findley's work is experimental in genre, style, and invention, and *The Telling of Lies* is no exception. Findley accepted the challenges of the mystery genre, worked within the confines of the murder plot, and found the excitement of writing, not in discovering what his characters would do, but in learning how they would react to events, how they would make things happen.

The murder in *The Telling of Lies*, particularly the suggestion that in some characters' minds it was a justified killing, brought out discussion of one of Findley's persistent themes. Over the years Findley has been asked why he is so fascinated by violence. In the Sandor interview, conducted shortly after publication of *The Telling of Lies*, he answered:

It is not that I am intrigued by violence; it is that I see it everywhere. I see it in ways that I guess do not always reach the page in other writers' works, and it is the violence we do to one another by behaving as we do: the violence of refusing to solve our problems, to confront our problems. Pride is a form of violence that is most of the basis of true violence. That physical violence comes from pride, fear, pigheadedness, greed. Instead of being merely the causes of violence, I see them as violence themselves. And so it is not necessarily that I am intrigued by violence, but that I am caught up in it. I cannot get away. That is my field as a writer. . . . Every single thing I have written hinges, turns, upon violence.

*The Telling of Lies* is Findley's most overtly political novel, articulating his apprehension of the ambiguous relations between the United States and Canada, and the danger of powerful governments and complacent citizens. One of the things that invoked Findley's anger before writing the novel was the disclosure of long-secret brainwashing experiments carried out in a Montreal psychiatric hospital during the 1950s by the U.S. Central Intelligence Agency with the Canadian government's knowledge. He saw this as an example of how the Canadian government cooperated with questionable American activities, as well as an instance when the Canadian people should have been aware of what was happening. Both these concerns are themes of *The Telling of Lies*. Writers, Findley believes, should criticize politicians, question the status quo, and reveal injustice.

Findley's apprehension of authoritarian governments, and his belief in the writer's duty to criticize them, began long before *The Telling of Lies*. His visit to the Soviet Union as a young actor, where he witnessed state control of the theatre, marked the inception of his belief that artists must have the freedom to express themselves without fear of censorship or reprisal, even when they criticize their government.

Another event, just a year or two after the trip to Russia, strengthened this belief. Findley was in Washington, District of Columbia, at the height of the Cold War and McCarthyism. Senator Joseph McCarthy had instigated a campaign to root out and harass Americans he considered Communist sympathizers. The House Committee on Un-American Activities investigated many artists and writers. Findley was in Washington at the time playwright Arthur Miller was being tried for refusing to cooperate with the committee and name people he had known at a Communist writers' meeting ten years earlier. Since Findley acted at night only, he was free to spend several days at the hearings. Miller eloquently defended the right of artists to voice their beliefs and opinions. "I am not here defending Communists," he declared. "I am here defending the right of an author to advocate, to write." The hearings had a profound effect on the young actor. " 'I never got over seeing him there,' " Findley told John Bemrose. " 'I was moved by his dignity, and his refusal to betray the people he knew by naming names.' "

Findley became a determined advocate of freedom for writers and, in 1987, served as president of the Canadian chapter of P.E.N. International. P.E.N. (Poets, Playwrights, Essayists, Editors, and Novelists) began as an international writers' club in 1921. In 1960, the Writers in Prison Committee was formed to deal exclusively with bringing aid — and, if possible, liberty — to imprisoned writers all over the world. As president of the Canadian chapter, Findley became a highly visible spokesperson for the international writing community.

Findley's involvement in P.E.N. became intensely personal when he started writing to an Ethiopian journalist, Martha Kumsa, who had been imprisoned in 1980. No formal charges were ever laid against Kumsa, and she was only allowed to see her three young children after seven years of imprisonment. Findley, his friend Jan Bauer, and others began a letter-writing campaign when she was adopted by P.E.N. as a prisoner of conscience. In her first reply, Kumsa addressed her letter to "Dear Mr. Kindley," unable to make out his difficult handwriting. Findley's letters always ended with "Hope against despair" or "Make prayers against despair."

Martha Kumsa was finally released from Central Prison in Addis Ababa in September 1989, and she and her children arrived in Canada as refugees two years later. For a P.E.N. benefit at the Winter Garden Theatre in Toronto, Findley and playwright Judith Thompson read a script he had written, an imaginary dialogue between Martha Kumsa and her minders — *minders* being the term used to describe those who take up the cause of a prisoner of conscience. In a dramatic and moving climax, Martha Kumsa walked onto the stage to the surprise and delight of the audience.

In a CBC Radio *Ideas* program, "Blue Is the Colour of Hope,"

Findley described their emotional meeting when Martha and her children arrived at Stone Orchard for Thanksgiving dinner:

> When she came — she's so small — when she came through the door, all we did was look at each other, hold each other, and then roar with laughter — dance in the hallway. We danced in the hallway! Coats were being taken off, the kids were running around, and Bill and Jan [Bauer] were there and we were all laughing. And I suddenly turned, damned serious, to Martha and said, "Hello, Martha." The thing is the words had not been said — the words had not been said.

Although Canadian writers are not imprisoned for their political or religious views, they often find their work repressed, and Findley has personally experienced the threat of censorship. As well as being unable to publish *Famous Last Words* in Britain while the Duchess of Windsor was alive, at various times Findley has seen his work come under attack. In 1991, a student in Sarnia, Ontario, campaigned to have *The Wars* removed from her high-school library. The passage to which she objected describes Robert Ross's rape by fellow officers. Rather than see the scene as symbolic of the psychological assault of war, the student charged that it promoted homosexuality.

In another instance, a poem that Findley wrote about federal revenue minister Otto Jelinek stopping homosexual literature at the border was removed from *Barbed Lyres*, a collection of satirical verse, presumably because the publisher feared a libel suit. The poem, ironically an anticensorship piece, was called "Otto-Eroticism" and was eventually published in *This Magazine*.

Books by fellow writers, such as Margaret Laurence, have also been attacked — and frequently banned from school libraries. These experiences have reinforced Findley's belief that writers must be free to express themselves within a free society. Findley is fond of quoting Salman Rushdie: "What does freedom of speech mean if it doesn't give you the licence to offend?"

*The Telling of Lies* was published in 1986 to a warm reception. Findley was by then an established writer whose new books were announced by his publisher and anticipated by critics, academics, and readers. Reviewers predictably discussed the novel as a mystery, awarding it varying degrees of success. Peter Moreira pointed out that the genre was an obvious choice for Findley, whose books "often start with an inexplicable situation and gradually reveal why and how the situation occurred." Other reviewers commented on the novel's prison imagery, declared Vanessa a success as a narrator, and — in Ken Adachi's words — forgave Findley his "playful indulgence" — the iceberg. *The Telling of Lies* won the Edgar Award from the Mystery Writers of America — a tribute to the novel's success in the mystery genre.

Another reading tour followed the novel's publication. Findley and Whitehead were away from Stone Orchard for two months as they travelled from St. John's to Victoria with stops at several schools and universities in smaller centres, as well as major cities in between. This time they travelled by air. Findley had recently overcome his reluctance to fly in order to fit lucrative Vancouver, Australia, and New Zealand speaking engagements into his busy schedule.

His phobia of flying dates from 1957, his second trip to Hollywood, when the airplane he was booked on crashed in the Grand Canyon, killing everyone on board. Findley arrived at the airport on the day of his scheduled flight only to discover that there was a problem with his work visa. A trip back into Toronto was necessary to straighten it out, and he missed the flight. After hearing about the crash on the news that night, he told me, he took a flight the following day "sailing on several martinis. I got totally pissed, and continued drinking on the plane. I was simply terrified. When I came home from California, I took the bus." He swore he would never fly again, and kept that promise for thirty years.

In 1982 Findley made a special trip to the Atlantic House Hotel. On a bright fall day he walked across the beach and down to the water, carrying his father's ashes. Allan Findley had recently died after a long illness. Findley threw the ashes to the wind and watched them fall back into the waves where his father had taught him to swim nearly fifty years earlier. He describes the moment in *Inside Memory*:

> So now I have put the rest of father's ashes in the sea and we have brought home a photograph which shows me doing this with the ashes making a kind of "rainbow" above where I am standing in the surf. It was a beautiful day, with an off-shore breeze and the sun very bright and the tide receding. Consequently, it was possible for me to walk a long way into the water and to have the confidence Father would be carried out to sea, not back to shore.

Findley's mother died in 1990. In *Inside Memory* he fondly recalls the last time his parents visited Stone Orchard together. They had sat side by side on a garden bench surrounded by spring flowers and bird song, reciting together a fragment from Euripides, *"Earth the most great and heaven on high"*:

> *Earth-gendered back to earth shall pass,*
> *And back to heaven the seeds of sky;*
> *Seeing all things into all may range*
> *And, sundering, show new shapes of change,*
> *But never that which is shall die.*

In place of a story, Findley's father had often recited poetry to his sons at bedtime, and Findley remembers hearing him recite this verse, but he had never heard his parents say it together. He used the last line of this fragment as the epigraph for *The Wars*.

# RADIO DRAMA

During the 1980s, CBC Radio listeners often heard Findley talking about his work, speaking out on issues of concern to writers, giving a moving tribute to a colleague, or reading an excerpt from his latest novel. He also continued to write radio documentary and drama. A four-part series on the life and music of Stephen Sondheim, written and narrated by Findley, and a radio drama, "The Trials of Ezra Pound," were broadcast in the late 1980s. In the latter production, which centred on Pound's imprisonment and trial for treason after World War II, Findley played the part of poet William Carlos Williams. *Morningside* presented three dramas based on stories in the *Stones* collection, as well as three Chekhov stories adapted by Findley for radio.

In 1988 his highly acclaimed adaptation of *Famous Last Words* was aired on both *Sunday Matinee* and *Stereo Theatre*. To adapt the novel to radio script, Findley nearly had to rewrite the book, juggling the numerous characters, devising new dialogue, dropping many of the prose passages, and creating bridges between scenes. Reviewer Robert Crew suggested that Findley's acting experience contributed to his success in adapting the prose narrative to effective drama.

Other reviewers and critics have also commented on the dramatic qualities of Findley's work, attributing it to his experience in the theatre. Cynthia Good noted that Findley's dialogue "contains the potential for ready conversion into a script: it is strong, realistic, immediate and, above all, dramatic." The reader is almost forced to read the lines aloud, becoming, as it were, an actor in the drama of the fiction. Findley has said he conceives of his fiction developing in scenes. He described the process to Stephen Godfrey:

> "I seem naturally to construct things in scenes, to have a sense of scene structure which can work on the stage. There are some things that a novel can do that a play can't — there is breadth of scope, a variety of narrative choices in a novel

— but the sense of character and the vividness of their voices can be effectively translated from a book to a play."

How else has Findley's theatre experience influenced his writing? He says that a sense of rhythm — Thornton Wilder's idea of a master rhythm — is the most valuable thing he brought from the stage to fiction writing. Readers, like actors, must be able to find their way easily through the words; if they cannot, he knows he does not yet have the perfect rhythm. He reads his work aloud — or Bill reads it to him — to see if the words flow smoothly.

In order to portray different characters successfully, Findley learned from directors and fellow actors how to *become* a person other than himself — an invaluable ability when creating fictional characters. Acting also taught him to supplant speech with gesture in both dramatic and prose work, to put fewer words on the page. In a CBC Television interview with Warren Davis, Findley called his acting years "an apprenticeship — almost a perfect apprenticeship for a writer."

## STONES

Findley's next work, *Stones*, was his second collection of short fiction. *Stones* contains nine stories, only four of them previously published. Originally the book was to include two more pieces, but as Findley was working on them, he gave up smoking for a few weeks. In the midst of withdrawal, he was unable to finish the stories. Findley continued to smoke despite several attempts to quit, and despite the loss of friends to lung cancer. In the photographs that grace dust jackets and accompany articles, he is invariably holding a cigarette in his right hand, like a prop; his languorous smoking gestures recall the world of the theatre.

The stories in *Stones* deal primarily with troubled family and personal relationships; most touch on madness, another of Findley's recurring themes. The focal point of the stories is Toronto's Queen Street Mental Health Centre, a series of low

FIGURE 16

*Toronto's Queen Street Mental Health Centre appears in nearly all the stories in* Stones, *as well as Findley's 1993 novel,* Headhunter.

brick buildings set amid grass and shrubbery on busy Queen Street West. Behind it are what remains of the Massey-Harris Company, a reminder of the Findley family past. Findley was startled when an editor pointed out that nearly all the stories in *Stones* had a reference to the Queen Street Centre. He knew it figured in some of them, but like rabbits and other "obsessions" in his earlier collection, it appears again and again as an ongoing motif, a metaphor for Toronto, the landscape where, in the past or present, his characters puzzle out their lives.

The collection's often-praised title story was conceived in 1987 when Findley and Bill Whitehead visited Dieppe after the discouraging *Famous Last Words* British tour. In the late 1970s they had written an award-winning television documentary about the survivors of this ill-planned and disastrous World War II battle, but Findley had never seen the site. The visit brought back to him the memory of a childhood friend whose father suffered a breakdown at Dieppe. In Findley's story a captain flees the battle when he sees the impossibility of driving the tanks on the loose stones of the beach. He lives the rest of his life branded as a coward, yet knowing he failed at an impossible task. When his tormented life is over, his son travels to Dieppe to scatter his father's ashes on the stones of the beach.


## BRAGG AND MINNA

The two Bragg and Minna stories that open *Stones* describe the unconventional marriage of two writers. Bragg is Findley's first overtly homosexual character since Adolphus Damarosch in *The Butterfly Plague*. Findley refuses to be called a homosexual writer and opposes the labelling of any group in society, whether based on gender, colour, nationality, or sexual orientation. He told Peter Buitenhuis, "I'm opposed to the ghettoization of homosexuals. 'Gay' is a word I loathe and detest. As a homosexual, it offends me deeply and it offends me twice deeply when other homosexuals choose that as an appellation — as an 'us against them' word. It's so confining. The point is to join the human race, as my mother would say." While Findley is an activist for gay rights and gay issues, he does not believe that everything he does should be defined by his homosexuality.

The Bragg and Minna stories are also an exploration of the difficult personal lives that writers often lead. Although the stories are not autobiographical, they are based, as Findley puts it, on the "tensions" and "wonders" of his long friendship with Marian Engel. Bragg is a "slow and careful" writer, whose favourite quotation is Gustave Flaubert's *"I spent the morning putting in a comma — and the afternoon taking it out."* Minna is prolific and undisciplined in her articulation of " 'all that noise' " she hears from the mad and half-mad on Queen Street West.

On an airplane coming back from Australia in 1986, Findley jotted down the story's opening sentences on a cigarette package:

> This is what Minna had written before she died:
> *Bragg always said we shouldn't have the baby and everything was done a man can do to prevent it. Still, I wanted her and she was born and now I realize I've given birth to all of Bragg's worst fears.*

Shortly before, at Ku-Ring-Gai, near Sidney, Findley saw the aboriginal rock carvings he described in "Bragg and Minna," including a small, bright-haired figure, one leg shorter than the other, six-fingered, flanked by a man and woman. A shaman figure, their guide explained. But, Findley told me emphatically, he disagreed: " 'That's their child,' I cried, 'and they are celebrating their wonderful, strange child.' " In Findley's story, Minna goes to Australia to live with her brain-damaged, six-fingered child, and later Bragg goes there to scatter Minna's ashes after she has died of cancer. After composing that first line, Findley lived with Bragg and Minna for a year before finally coming to terms with them on paper.

Over the many years of their friendship, Findley and Marian Engel continually discussed their writing. After *Not Wanted on the Voyage* was published, Marian scribbled him a note that ended, "You shook your fist at God!" It remains Findley's favourite comment on the novel: "Marian had a great sense of humour," he told me, "and she was putting me in my place." When Engel died in 1985, Findley wrote an affectionate tribute to her, adding her own thoughts on writing as she neared the end of a long battle with cancer. "In Memoriam" concludes with Engel's words:

> Time has done some work. We shall see if it is good or ill that has been produced, if impatience has been replaced by wisdom, and lack of energy replaced by richness. Anything could happen. I write because I have always written. I try again because I don't know what else to do. It is both a trial and a joy.

For Findley too, a trial and a joy.

*Stones* was received with enthusiasm and won the prestigious Trillium Award for outstanding work by an Ontario author. Findley adapted three of the stories for broadcast on CBC Radio's *Morningside* and joined actors for a dramatic reading of "Stones" produced by Paul Thompson at the Vancouver Writers Festival. Reviewers thought the stories in the collection carefully crafted and unified in theme. Each one, wrote Barbara Novak, "touches in some way on madness, on the anguish of perceiving the world, or oneself, in a particularly harsh and unforgiving light." The horror of the characters' condition, however, is mitigated by their human capacity for love.

Findley's short fiction has been called magic realism, a term he claims not to understand, much less identify with. Although his writing has also been discussed as postmodern and deconstructionist, Findley has consistently resisted labels, genres, and schools, explaining that the voice and characters come first, that he never sits down to write in a particular style or mode. The result is work that defies categories and expectations.

When *Inside Memory: Pages from a Writer's Workbook* appeared in 1990, Findley once again surprised critics and readers. The work is neither an autobiography, nor a memoir, nor a collection of essays. It is an assortment of journal entries, articles, radio pieces, speeches, and stories about friends and colleagues; it includes an interview with Bill entitled "Alice Drops Her Cigarette on the Floor . . ." and a scene cut from *Famous Last Words*. The volume is a pastiche of experiences and ideas rather than a carefully structured accounting of Findley's life. It is also, as Val Ross points out, more about others than about Findley himself. The personal passages are skilfully paced with amusing stories and engaging recollections about writers and friends. Ross suggests that in this work Findley — the ex-actor, the storyteller — is masked, less open than he seems.

When old friends Stan and Nancy Colbert of HarperCollins first suggested the idea of a memoir to Findley, he was adamantly opposed. Bill, having organized the many boxes of Findley's papers before sending them to the National Archives, recognized the validity of the Colberts' idea, and talked Findley into at least looking at his thirty years of journals, letters, and articles. In the three days they spent in the Archives' reading room in Ottawa, Findley discovered a wealth of stories about people he had known during his years of acting and writing. The journal entries triggered more memories, and Findley became intrigued with the project: it would be an opportunity for the storyteller to explore his memories and bring together some of the stories from his life. Findley writes in the first few pages of *Inside Memory* that the act of remembering is a form of hope; it entails making peace with time; memory is survival.

The book is roughly organized around the writing of each of Findley's first six novels, with a section on his acting career, and one on Stone Orchard. The final segment contains eulogies to several friends and colleagues and a speech entitled "My Final Hour." The closing words of the speech — and of the book —

are "Goodbye. And thank you." This conclusion led more than one interviewer to ask if it were Findley's final book, his farewell. Definitely not, he assured T.J. Collins. It was, rather, written at a turning point in Findley's life, providing a "summing up of where I've been so far." After publication of *Inside Memory*, Findley was again named Author of the Year by the Canadian Authors Association, the first two-time winner of that honour.

## NOT WANTED ON THE STAGE

In the early 1990s Findley saw one of his novels turned into a successful stage play. He is surprised that *Not Wanted on the Voyage* was the first of his novels to be made into a play, having thought *The Wars* or *Famous Last Words* more likely candidates. But shortly after *Not Wanted on the Voyage* was published, Robin Phillips, then at the Stratford Festival, acquired the rights and started workshops with the Young Company.

Findley has kept up his association with Stratford since his participation as an actor in the 1953 opening season. He often attends performances and has written program notes and articles. In 1987 he returned as "almost a playwright" to watch the Young Company workshop his novel and was pleased with the results. But when Phillips left Stratford, the project was dropped. Fortunately, Richard Rose, artistic director of Toronto's Necessary Angel Theatre Company, had been interested in *Not Wanted on the Voyage* from the beginning and took on the project. Rose and scriptwriter D.D. Kugler spent two years adapting the novel for the stage before it was workshopped and rewritten at the National Theatre School in Montreal in 1991. It opened in Winnipeg and Toronto early in 1992.

Throughout the process, Findley gave his support and encouragement, but his involvement in the project was indirect. From his recent experience adapting *Famous Last Words* for radio, he knew that a vast amount of cutting and revision would be needed to prepare *Not Wanted on the Voyage* for the stage. Rose and Kugler solicited suggestions and asked Findley to read early drafts of the play. At one point he told them not to be so reverential, to "cut themselves free" from the book. When they did so, the play began to take on a life of its own. Still, watching the new creation emerge was not always easy. When the character Crowe was cut from the script, it was, as Findley put it, like cutting off a hand. He was also concerned that singing sheep, faeries, and unicorns — while believable on the page — would merely appear cute on the stage.

Findley's approval of Rose and Kugler's adaptation, however, became obvious at a benefit reading before the play went into production. A group of actors, friends, and supporters of the Necessary Angel Theatre Company gathered on board the *Captain Matthew Flinders* in Toronto Harbour on a mild March evening. As the ship cruised Lake Ontario — the lights of Toronto's skyline adding a bit of magic to the voyage — the actors began to read. Findley, sitting beside Bill at a table near the makeshift stage, listened intently. Some of the audience — including myself — unable to hear over the noise of the throbbing engines, had gathered behind the actors, forming an ersatz Greek chorus. We not only had the advantage of being on stage with the actors, but also of watching Findley's delighted reaction to the rebirth of one of his creations.

Although objection to Findley's interpretation of the story of Noah and the Ark had been mild when the novel was published, it was quite another matter when the novel became a play. The controversy began even before opening night at the Manitoba Theatre Centre. After CBC Television broadcast a documentary in Winnipeg about the making of the play that included scenes from the production, their call-in lines were immediately inundated. The callers were angry, many hostile. They labelled the play insulting, blasphemous, sacrilegious, and several insisted it be banned. One caller, the self-proclaimed leader of the province's Ku Klux Klan, said that when his group came to power, people like Timothy Findley would be shot. On opening night, some audience members walked out of the performance; others left at intermission; a few cancelled their season's subscription. The Manitoba Justice Department investigated audience complaints, but no charges were laid.

Despite the controversy, the play received respectful reviews and the Manitoba Theatre Centre was commended for staging it. After the Winnipeg run, the play was shortened, a few changes made, and the production moved to an uneventful run in Toronto. The cast, which included Janet Wright, Roland Hewgill, Goldie Semple, and Anne Anglin, was highly praised in reviews, as were the staging and sets. But like *Can You See Me Yet?*, the play itself was considered difficult and disturbing. Liam Lacey, writing in the *Globe and Mail*, called it "a flashy, but ultimately empty, form of fist-shaking at the big straw man in the sky." Findley, however, as well as his fans, found it " 'stunning.' "


## LIFE AT STONE ORCHARD

Timothy Findley continues to live and work at Stone Orchard where he and Bill Whitehead recently celebrated thirty years together. Both writers are in their early sixties. Bill recently retired from television-documentary writing; now only one writer at Stone Orchard has deadlines to meet.

The farmhouse is surrounded by flower and vegetable gardens; a pond, complete with an island, is the latest landscaping addition. Cats doze on the sunny veranda, and out the kitchen window cows graze peacefully in the field across the road. Upstairs, the writer is at work, while downstairs in his office, Bill taps away at the computer.

With financial security, recognition of his literary talent, and the stability of life at Stone Orchard, Findley's sixth decade has brought him a measure of tranquillity. He continues to drink, but more moderately, and is usually monitored by Bill. Less frequently immersed in inner turmoil, Findley now finds he can become more involved in the lives of those close to him. He generously makes time in his busy life to see researchers and young writers, to share the lives of Len and Anne Collins and their family across the road, and to enjoy the rolling fields and woods of the countryside. He and Bill speak with warmth and appreciation of Cannington friends and neighbours. Their lives at Stone Orchard, Findley says, have been enriched by long association with two special people: their neighbour and house-keeper, "the glorious Nora Joyce," and Len Collins, "whom we call the miracle worker." Len's skills are evident in both house and garden. It was he who renovated the kitchen; constructed the Victorian gazebo in the garden; designed and built the addi-tion that houses the studio and Findley's retreat; and knew exactly what was needed when Findley asked him for "a desk worthy of a writer." The result of this last request is a magni-ficent piece of furniture that takes up nearly half of Findley's book-lined workroom.

Over the years a succession of high-school boys have been hired to do yard work, animal care, and errands — a position coveted by local students. The perks of the job might include a night of theatre in Toronto, introduction to ethnic cuisine, help with homework, and a chance to pursue their own particular interests. One of them spent a summer constructing a stone path and patio under the honey locusts east of the house. Because his name was Scott Bryan, that part of the garden is now known as "Scottland." Each of the students has contributed something special and become a part of the Stone Orchard family.

A recent CBC-NFB film, *Timothy Findley: Anatomy of a Writer*, is both an intimate portrait of Findley's day-to-day life and a rare insight into the writer at work. In this production, Findley describes his love for the land of his ancestors and for the animals that share his life, talks candidly about his alcoholism and homo-sexuality, and tells stories — about his grandmother, Ruth Gor-don, his father, and himself. Findley the actor is very much in evidence as he adopts the roles of his stories' characters. The film opens with an appropriately-attired Findley, the academic, inter-viewing Findley, the writer.

Much of the film focuses on Findley's writing process. He

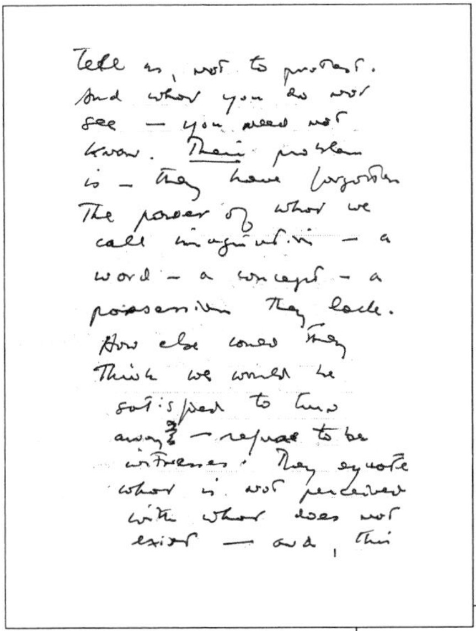

Tell us, not to protest. And what you do not see — you need not know. Their problem is — they have forgotten the power of what we call imagination — a word — a concept — a possession they lack. How else could they think we would be satisfied to turn away? — refuse to be witnesses? They equate what is not perceived with what does not exist — and, this

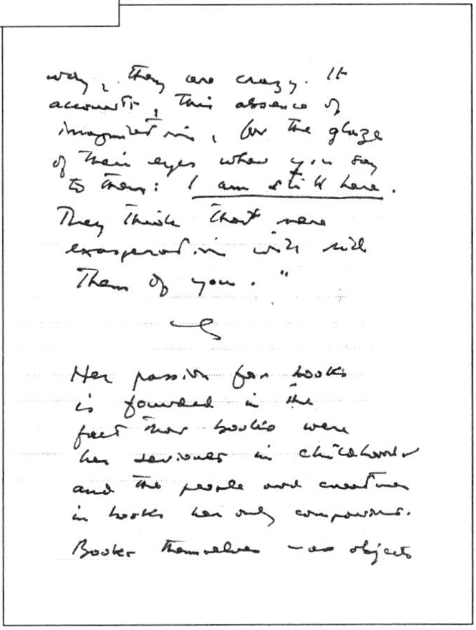

way, they are crazy. It accounts, this absence of imagination, for the glaze of their eyes when you say to them: I am still here. They think that mere exasperation will rid them of you."

Her passion for books is founded in the fact that books were her saviours in childhood and the people and creatures in books her only companions. Books themselves — as objects

FIGURE 17

*Two pages from Findley's* Headhunter *notebook recording ideas about imagination and describing Lilah Kemp's passion for books.*

writes in longhand, working from notebooks in which he records ideas and scenes. Bill Whitehead then uses a word processor to type the second or third draft of each chapter or section. In one scene from the film, Bill reads to Findley the opening of a short story, inserting some deliberate and hilarious mistakes; then, more seriously, he questions the choice of words in another passage: "Hose? Don't you mean socks?"

In the film, Findley tells how ideas for stories come to him — often as fully formed characters "screaming to be let out" — and he reads an excerpt from his journal about a man who talks to his vegetables, a scene that was later to find its way into *Headhunter*. In a unique sequence illustrating Findley's creative process, William Hutt, Martha Henry, and Susan Coyne act out a scene from a play Findley is working on. "That's wrong," Findley says, and rewrites the scene. The actors replay it. "That's still not right," he says, and reworks it yet again. The actors interpret four versions in all.

## THE STILLBORN LOVER

The play mentioned above is Findley's *The Stillborn Lover*, which premièred in March 1993 at the Grand Theatre in London, Ontario. The genesis of *The Stillborn Lover* goes back many years and has its basis in factual events. True stories and real people often inform and inspire Findley's work. For this play, the facts concern two Canadian diplomats, John Watkins and Herbert Norman, both of whom died while under investigation during the Cold War years.

Herbert Norman had associated with Communists while at Cambridge; John Watkins was a homosexual. Watkins died of a heart attack during interrogation by the RCMP. Norman jumped to his death in Cairo after his name was brought up yet again during the U.S. House Committee on Un-American Activities hearings. Both were betrayed, in Findley's view, by the government leaders they served. Neither was a traitor.

Findley was deeply angered by revelations of what he felt was a CIA-RCMP witch-hunt to hound homosexuals out of the diplomatic service. He was equally angered by government leaders' betrayal of the two diplomats. Although Findley had these cases in mind, Harry Raymond in *The Stillborn Lover* is neither Norman nor Watkins; like all of Findley's fictional characters, he is the product of Findley's imagination: a figure uniquely himself.

In the play, Canadian Ambassador Raymond is recalled from Russia for questioning after a young Russian is found dead in a Moscow hotel room. The dead man was the ambassador's lover. Marian, the ambassador's wife, suffers from Alzheimer's disease. Her memory is unreliable, her involvement in her husband's intrigue unclear. Her mental confusion may be authentic, or simply convenient.

Findley has had personal experience with Alzheimer's, having watched it affect people close to him, including Bill's mother. Although it destroys memory — so important to a writer — the disease has another side. As Findley explained to Julie Hobson, "the other aspect of Alzheimer's is that there are these wonderful flights of free creation where you create a whole scene out of memory. The memory is whole or complete in itself and you draw whoever's there with you into that place." Marian Raymond's creation of such a memory, concerning a tree in the garden, is the image that first set Findley's mind to work on what became *The Stillborn Lover*.

Some of Marian's memories take the audience to Nagasaki, just after the second atomic bomb destroyed the Japanese city where the Raymonds met, honeymooned, and returned for the birth of their child. The Japanese-style set and the recurring theme of the game of Go accentuate the past. Nagasaki — the word is repeated throughout the play — symbolizes the destruction caused by acts of power untempered by moral decency.

Findley has long admired Japanese culture and literature. He often gives as a gift the eleventh-century Japanese work, *The Pillow Book of Sei Shōnagon*, and says its author was an inspiration for some of the traits of Vanessa in *The Telling of Lies*, another

Findley work influenced by Japanese culture. He talked to Suzanne Sandor about that influence:

Also, quite by chance I came upon a book called *The Narrow Road to the Deep North* by a Japanese poet called Basho, and it is a classic tale of journeys. I found myself enchanted with the whole way of presenting why we do things — the most important things in our lives are presented with the coolest possible voice, yet it still carries the weight of devastation. It swept me away, not necessarily into the culture, but into the way of seeing. It was very much the writer in me having discovered a way of writing and presenting story and viewpoint that matched what I wanted to achieve myself.

*The Stillborn Lover* stars William Hutt as the ambassador and Martha Henry as his wife. In fact, it was written for them. When the actors were asked to perform some scenes for the NFB film about Findley, they thought the excerpts were from a new novel. Henry, discovering they were from a play, wanted to produce it at the Grand Theatre where she is artistic director. In March 1992, she announced that it would be part of the 1992–93 season.

Findley told Patricia Black that writing *The Stillborn Lover* was one of the most extraordinary writing experiences he has ever had. Although an excerpt from it, entitled "Inquest," had appeared in *Books in Canada* in 1989, only a few scenes had been written by July 1992. Findley worked furiously — at the same time he was trying to finish the manuscript of *Headhunter* — to have a preliminary script ready for the first read-through in August. He completed the script in just three weeks, pulling together the images and scenes that had been in his mind for four years.

## A THEATRE REUNION

The reading of *The Stillborn Lover* that took place in Martha Henry's kitchen in Stratford was something of a reunion for the group gathered there. Findley had worked with William Hutt

FIGURE 18

*Playwright, director, and actors confer on the set of*
The Stillborn Lover. *Seated, from left: Timothy Findley,*
*William Hutt, and Martha Henry. Standing: Peter Moss.*

since the late 1940s, acted at Stratford with him, and had written the two John A. Macdonald roles for him. Hutt had also acted in the film version of *The Wars*, as had Martha Henry. Findley first met Henry when he interviewed her for the CBC Radio series, *Taping Stratford*, in the 1960s. He remembers their long, pleasant conversations with affection.

Findley has long admired the two actors. He told Patricia Black he considers them "two of the great actors of this time in the English-speaking world." Peter Moss, who directed *The Stillborn Lover*, was also an old colleague. Fourteen years earlier he had directed *John A. — Himself!* on the Grand stage. There were other past associates too. One of the actors, Hardee T. Lineham, had played a part in *The Wars*, and another, Donald Davis, had been in "The Trials of Ezra Pound" and played Yaweh in the Necessary Angel Theatre benefit reading of *Not Wanted on the Voyage*.

Findley and Bill Whitehead spent two weeks in London, Ontario, while the play was in rehearsal. Findley watched and made suggestions as his characters came to life on stage. The director and actors made their own suggestions, and the play gradually took shape. Patricia Black asked Findley how he felt watching rehearsals:

> It *is* the best time. A lot of the actors have said this — rehearsing is the best time, because that's when who you are as an artist is at its peak, the exploration and the ability to explore further, the willingness to be so daring that you'll go anywhere to find the person, to make a fool of yourself and get it wrong. The process is absolutely wonderful.

Clearly the ex-actor in Findley was back on the stage.

After a successful run at the Grand, the production went on to Ottawa's National Arts Centre, the coproducer of the play. A radio version was broadcast and the script published. The play received favourable reviews. The *Globe and Mail*'s H.J. Kirchhoff praised its "stellar cast" and declared it "a superb production." Doug Bale wrote:

Besides scenes of outwardly casual exchanges and of heated confrontations there are long moments of near-stillness into which the next words, when they finally do come, fall like bombs. One realizes early that every word in this play has been expertly chosen for precise effect.

*The Stillborn Lover* signals Findley's return to writing drama, a form that for him has proved less successful than his novels and short stories, but which has always been close to his actor's heart. In a 1988 interview, Peter Buitenhuis asked Findley why he did not write more drama. "I have," he said, "but it's all in drawers. I'm not happy with myself as a playwright yet."

## HEADHUNTER

Findley's seventh novel, *Headhunter*, was released while *The Stillborn Lover* was playing in London, prompting Doug Bale to call the feat a "literary doubleheader." Indeed, 1993 was a banner year for Findley, bringing to fruition several years of work. He saw the production of his most successful play and received acclaim for *Headhunter*, his first novel since *The Telling of Lies*, seven years earlier.

For years, Findley told me, whenever people asked him what he was working on, he would tell them he was writing *Heart of Darkness* set in Rosedale, "and everybody would laugh, including me." True enough, like Joseph Conrad's *Heart of Darkness*, *Headhunter* has a character named Kurtz. The novel begins:

On a winter's day, while a blizzard raged through the streets of Toronto, Lilah Kemp inadvertently set Kurtz free from page 92 of *Heart of Darkness*. Horror-stricken, she tried to force him back between the covers. The escape took place at the Metropolitan Toronto Reference Library, where Lilah Kemp sat reading beside the rock pool. She had not even said *come forth*, but there Kurtz stood before her, framed by the woven jungle of cotton trees and vines that passed for botanic atmosphere.

"Get in," Lilah pleaded — whispering and holding out the book. But Kurtz ignored her and stepped away.

Luckily, a Dr. Marlow soon appears and moves in next door to Lilah. She has faith that Marlow can save them all from Kurtz.

Rosedale is one of the areas of Toronto depicted in the novel, a Toronto of the near future where AIDS and a new epidemic, said to be spread by starlings, are rampant; where moral and sexual taboos have disappeared; where the environment, and life itself, are threatened. The upper-class enclave of Findley's childhood may seem an incongruous location for the evils he depicts. He told John Bemrose, however, that "in truth, I've always thought of Rosedale as one of the river-stations Conrad writes about — one of the points on the journey to the heart of darkness."

The environs of Queen Street West, familiar territory from Findley's *Stones* stories, provide a contrasting, yet complementary, setting to Rosedale. Many of the characters are either patients or doctors at the Queen Street Mental Health Centre or at the "Parkin Institute," an institution closely modelled on Toronto's Clarke Institute of Psychiatry. Not surprisingly, Philip Marchand has interpreted *Headhunter* as an attack on the abuses of psychiatry. Rupert Kurtz, the brilliant and amoral director of the Parkin Institute, is involved in questionable drug experiments on patients and has connections to a secret group of men that recruits teenagers for sexual use, and abuse.

Readers know of Findley's affinity for those whom society labels mad, for such characters appear in many of his novels and short stories. Findley believes that some mental disturbances, like schizophrenia, provide a means of perception denied to ordinary people. He told Philip Marchand, " 'In some cases you have to offer a patient the gift of the madness — and it is a gift. . . . What if we took madness away from what is regarded in all cultures as the shaman? It's merely a route. It's a route to perception.' "

There is schizophrenia in Findley's family background, and he told Marchand that he believes himself prone to similar mild disturbances. " 'I tend to believe that I'm schizophrenic, but I'm lucky because it defines itself, in my case, as writing,' " he said. " 'It doesn't define itself as damaging episodes.' " Lilah, a former librarian who evokes characters from the pages of books, is "mad," as is Amy Wylie, a poet in the novel. Dr. Marlow recognizes that madness is a gift both women have.

In "Alice Drops Her Cigarette on the Floor . . . ," Findley explains the origin of his perception of insanity as a creative force. When he was just six or seven, a member of his family was placed in a mental institution:

> And my perception of this person was that she was brilliant — that she had incredible insights into what was really going on in the world around us. . . . [I]t struck me that I should listen. To this person who was close to me, who was sitting in the room with me. . . . Her perception of the world was clarified through a route of her own that was special: that was unique . . . and maybe dangerous to other people. . . . She could see the heart of things. . . . [she] tampered with the protective walls thrown up by other people to keep the hurt of reality out.

Findley dedicated *Headhunter* to R.E. Turner, the psychiatrist who helped him delve into his own darkness to find what was hidden there, to uncover the lies that hold a troubled psyche together. He described the process to Peter Gzowski on *Morningside*, explaining how such self-analysis enables a person to break free. Findley believes the novelist and psychiatrist share a common role: both can lead us down into the dark — into the heart of darkness — and then back out, into the light. In a sense, they both play the role of Orpheus.

Many literary characters — in addition to Kurtz and Marlow — people the Toronto of *Headhunter*, characters that recall

Emma Bovary, Jay Gatsby, Jekyll and Hyde, and even Grendel. Lilah Kemp talks to Susanna Moodie and keeps a copy of *Wuthering Heights* in the baby buggy she pushes around with her. Peter Rabbit's shoes — she once conjured him from the pages of Beatrix Potter's book — are her talisman. Literary references, engaging characters, and humorous moments lighten what would be an otherwise unbearably dark story. As well, Findley's editor convinced him to make the ending less bleak, to leave the reader with some hope. Like Marlow, Findley does lead us out of his "Heart of Darkness."

## AGAINST DESPAIR

With the completion of *The Stillborn Lover* and *Headhunter*, and a welcome respite from deadlines, Findley made another attempt to give up smoking, having determined at last to quit. " 'I've lost one of my best friends,' " he told Philip Marchand

"Seriously. The companion at the writing desk. And it was wonderful for helping to breach those social moments that were awkward or full of tension.

"I'm not a party boy — never was. So it's difficult for me to go to a party — but you have to if you're in this business — all of this is now part of your work, in a sense. And without cigarettes I'm finding it *appallingly* difficult."

Invariably, interviewers ask "What's next?" as soon as a writer's latest book is published. Findley currently speaks of two projects: a play, *Other People's Children*, based on a television script from the early 1980s, and a new novel, tentatively titled *Pilgrim*. About the novel, he doesn't like to say much: "Novels always seem to start out to be one thing, and end up another," he told me, but Bill Whitehead hints that it is about a writer who makes a pilgrimage. "Everyone will think the writer is T.F., but he isn't."

Findley was recently asked if he is afraid he will run out of material. On the contrary — he is afraid he will not live long enough to get everything in his head down on paper. Findley made this comment in *Timothy Findley: Anatomy of a Writer*, a film Dave Wesley says "goes a long way in giving us a glimpse at who Findley is. . . ." Directed by Terence Macartney-Filgate, the film won the Donald Brittain Award for best documentary program early in 1993. Wesley proceeds to praise the film for capturing this "tremendously caring and inventive human being, whose innate sense of life's wonder and theatricality hasn't dissolved his willingness to peer into its darker corners."

Timothy Findley is familiar with life's darker corners; he has glimpsed them in the Dachau photographs, in wars, fascist movements, mental hospitals, and prison camps — and in his own life. But Findley's writing is a confirmation of his belief that the human imagination can illuminate these dark spaces. In "My Final Hour," the speech he gave to the Philosophy Society at Trent University, Findley told his audience, "Nothing is harder, now in this present time, than staring down despair. But stare it down we must." To cheer Martha Kumsa in prison, he had offered a similar belief: "Make prayers against despair," "Hope against despair." Scribbled beneath his signature in my copy of *Not Wanted on the Voyage* are the words "Against Despair."

The last story of these "stories from a life," of Timothy Findley's life, is reserved for the biographer.

When I visited Stone Orchard in the summer of 1992, Findley and I were talking of the books we'd enjoyed as children, and I mentioned Beatrix Potter's animal stories. Findley responded enthusiastically:

Oh, yes, of course, wonderful stuff . . . and I fervently believe that *The Tale of Peter Rabbit* is one of the great English novels. It is a perfect model for how to tell a story from an innovative point of view. It isn't just the story of a rabbit going to look for lettuces; it is the story told from the rabbit's point of view. . . . Peter Rabbit is a *stunning* piece of work — such wonderful things like "lippity-lippity" and the image of Peter and the radish. Just look at the picture of

Peter eating the radish. He is in ecstasy . . . *his toes are curling,* one little foot over the other . . . like this. . . .

With that he leapt from the chesterfield and, cigarette still in hand, struck Peter's pose, up on tiptoe, feet crossed one over the other, toes curled in radish ecstasy — the dancer / actor still.

Then he threw back his head in delighted, long laughter. Against despair.

# CHRONOLOGY

1930 On 30 October, Timothy Irving Frederick Findley is born to Allan and Margaret Findley. The family is forced to leave Toronto's prestigious Rosedale area for a time when the Depression erodes stockbroker Allan Findley's financial capital.

1939 World War II begins. Allan joins the air force and Margaret struggles to keep the family together. Findley and older brother Michael briefly attend a private school, St. Andrew's College. Childhood is marred by illness, separation, loneliness, and the deaths of an infant brother and Uncle Tif, a World War I hero.

1945 Findley graduates from Rosedale Public School. He announces to his family that he is homosexual.

1946 He attends Jarvis Collegiate off and on, leaving at seventeen without graduating. A tutor is engaged. Findley writes long, romantic novels in bed while recovering from illness.

1947 Findley works as a labourer at the Massey-Harris Company to pay for ballet lessons.

1950 Illness recurs and Findley's parents send him on a recuperative voyage to Switzerland.

1948–52 When back problems rule out dancing, Findley turns to acting, appearing in stage plays and on television, playing the role of Peter Pupkin in CBC Television's production of Stephen Leacock's *Sunshine Sketches of a Little Town*.

1953 Findley gets a break in acting. He is cast in two productions of the Stratford Shakespeare Festival's first season, working with Tyrone Guthrie and Alec Guinness.

Guinness sponsors Findley at the Central School of Speech and Drama in London, England.

1954 Findley is part of the British Company of Thornton Wilder's *The Matchmaker* and gains the friendship of Wilder and actress Ruth Gordon, who both encourage him to write. Findley writes his first short story, "About Effie," in response to a challenge from Gordon.

1955 In London, Findley works as a contract actor for British theatre producer H.M. Tennent, appearing in several productions. Findley goes to the Soviet Union with Peter Brook's production of *Hamlet*.

1956 "About Effie" is published in the first issue of *Tamarack Review* while Findley is on tour in North America with *The Matchmaker*.

1956–58 Findley makes two trips to Hollywood: the first an unsuccessful attempt to pursue his acting career and the second to do script work for the *Playhouse 90* television series. When his own script is rejected, Findley becomes discouraged about a career in movies and television.

1958 Findley returns to Toronto where he acts on CBC Television and in stage productions. He meets actress Janet Reid and, despite his professed homosexuality, marries her. Their brief marriage is amicably annulled. Findley is depressed and drinking heavily.

1962–63 He meets actor and documentary-writer William Whitehead. They rent Findley's parents' house in Richmond Hill and both retire from the theatre. Findley writes advertising copy for a local radio station, the arts news for CBC Radio's *The Learning Stage*, and works on his first novel, *The Last of the Crazy People*.

1964 Findley and Whitehead buy a farm near Cannington, Ontario, which they name Stone Orchard. The farm is near the area where Findley's ancestors settled in the 1840s. Findley writes extensively for CBC Radio and Television.

1967      *The Last of the Crazy People* is published in New York after being rejected by several Canadian publishers. Findley works on two screenplays: *The Paper People*, CBC Television's first full-length colour film, and *Don't Let the Angels Fall*, for the National Film Board. Both are disappointing experiences.

1969      Findley's second novel, *The Butterfly Plague*, set in Hollywood and Nazi Germany, is dismissed by Canadian presses and published in the United States. Only two reviews are published in Canada. Findley is depressed by this lack of recognition. He and Whitehead spend the summer driving and camping across the United States and Canada's Northwest Territories.

1971–74      Findley concentrates on writing for television, becoming chief writer for *The Whiteoaks of Jalna* series and collaborating with Whitehead on the award-winning script for *The National Dream*. He helps found the Writers' Union of Canada.

1974      Findley becomes the National Arts Centre's first playwright-in-residence. In Ottawa he works on his script for *Can You See Me Yet?*, which is produced the following season and generally dismissed. He begins writing *The Wars*, set in World War I, using his Uncle Tif's letters as research material.

1977      *The Wars* is published in Canada to high praise and wins the Governor General's Award. Findley is finally recognized as a major writer at a time of renewed interest and activity in Canadian literature.

1978      He enjoys the friendship and support of other Canadian writers, serves as chairman of the Writers' Union of Canada, and is appointed writer-in-residence at the University of Toronto.

1979      Findley's play, *John A. — Himself!*, about Canada's first prime minister and starring William Hutt, is produced at Theatre London, London, Ontario.

1981      *Famous Last Words*, set in World War II Europe, is published and received with great acclaim. This ambitious, panoramic novel had taken four years to write.

1982    Findley receives an honorary degree from Trent University. Findley's father dies.

1983    Increased critical interest in Findley's work leads to a reissue of *The Last of the Crazy People*. *The Wars* is made into a film with Stratford veteran Robin Phillips directing. It includes a cast of well-known Canadian stage actors and music composed by Glenn Gould.

1984    Findley's first collection of short stories, *Dinner Along the Amazon*, is published. It contains stories written throughout his career, including his first, "About Effie." He receives an honorary degree from the University of Guelph.

1985    Findley's fifth novel, *Not Wanted on the Voyage*, an imaginative retelling of the story of Noah and the Ark, appears to enthusiastic reviews. He wins a Canadian Authors Association Award and is writer-in-residence at the University of Winnipeg.

1986    A revised edition of *The Butterfly Plague* and a new novel, *The Telling of Lies*, a mystery with a political theme and a female protagonist, are published. Findley is made an Officer of the Order of Canada and serves as Canadian president of P.E.N. International.

1987    *Famous Last Words* is published in Britain after the death of the Duchess of Windsor. Attacks on Findley's portrayal of the Windsors boost the novel's sales but distress Findley. He and Whitehead holiday in Dieppe, the scene of an earlier television script and a later short story.

1988    *Stones*, Findley's second collection of short fiction, appears. It contains stories written during the 1980s, including the Bragg and Minna stories, and receives the Ontario Trillium Award. Findley is interviewed, written about, and heard on CBC Radio. His five-part radio adaptation of *Famous Last Words* is broadcast.

| 1990 | *Inside Memory: Pages from a Writer's Workbook*, a collection of articles, journal entries, and reminiscences, is published. Findley's mother dies. |
| 1991 | He receives his second Canadian Authors Association Award for *Inside Memory* and is named to the Order of Ontario. |
| 1992 | *Not Wanted on the Voyage* is made into a play and produced in Winnipeg and Toronto. The National Film Board makes a film about Findley's life and writing methods. |
| 1993 | A play written for Martha Henry and William Hutt, *The Stillborn Lover*, is produced at the Grand Theatre in London, Ontario. Findley's seventh novel, *Headhunter*, is published. Findley and Bill Whitehead continue to live and work at Stone Orchard. |

# WORKS CONSULTED

Adachi, Ken. "Lies and Secrets Hiding Inside Family Relations." Rev. of *The Telling of Lies*, by Timothy Findley. *Toronto Star* 25 Oct. 1986: M4.

Ashley, Audrey M. "Odd Mix of Styles Confuses Audience." *Citizen* [Ottawa] 5 Feb. 1979: 27.

Bale, Doug. "Findley's *Stillborn Lover* Superb." Rev. of *The Stillborn Lover*, by Timothy Findley. Grand Theatre, London, ON. *London Free Press* 27 Mar. 1993: D9.

———. "*John A. — Himself!* Potentially Fine Play." Rev. of *John A. — Himself!*, by Timothy Findley. Theatre London, London, ON. *London Free Press* 1 Feb. 1979: C5.

———. "A Literary Doubleheader." *London Free Press* 26 Mar. 1993: C1.

———. "Next Theatre London Play Revives Era of Macdonald." *London Free Press* 24 Jan. 1979: D9.

Bemrose, John. "Two Spring Hits." *Maclean's* 19 Apr. 1993: 49–50.

Blackadar, Bruce. "Findley and the Rise of Fascism." *Toronto Star* 22 Oct. 1981: F1.

"Blue Is the Colour of Hope." Prod. Marilyn Powell. *Ideas*. CBC Radio, Toronto. 15–16 June 1992.

Cameron, Elspeth. "The Inner Wars of Timothy Findley." *Saturday Night* Jan. 1985: 24–33.

Collins, T.J. "The Writing Life: Timothy Findley." *Canadian Author and Bookman* 66.4 (1991): 3–5.

Crew, Robert. "*Famous Last Words* Makes Smooth Transition to Radio." *Toronto Star* 9 Jan. 1988: F3.

Cusack, Veronica. "Timothy Findley Lives Here." *Toronto Life* Apr. 1993: 74–79.

Denison, Merrill. *Harvest Triumphant: The Story of Massey-Harris*. Toronto: McClelland, 1948.

Dunphy, Catherine. "Timothy Findley Loves the Slow Lane." *Toronto Star* 29 July 1988, "Life": D1+.

Edwards, Thomas R. "The Grim War and the Great War." Rev. of *Better Times Than These*, by Winston Groom; and *The Wars*, by Timothy Findley. *New York Times Book Review* 9 July 1978: 14+.

Engel, Marian. Rev. of *The Butterfly Plague*, by Timothy Findley. *Telegram* [Toronto] 13 May 1969, sec. 3: 5.

——. "The Year of the Novel Brings a Grab-Bag." Rev. of *Bullet Park*, by John Cheever; *Mr. Bridge*, by Evan S. Connell; *Make Yourself an Earthquake*, by Mark Dintenfass; *The Butterfly Plague*, by Timothy Findley; and *Terra Amata*, by J.M.G. LeClizio. *Toronto Star* 19 Apr. 1969: 30.

F., J. "The Sound of Writers Reading." *Globe and Mail* 28 May 1983, "Fanfare": 2.

Findley, Thomas Irving. Letters. Private collection of Timothy Findley.

Findley, Timothy. "Alarms and Excursions: Some Adventures in the Book Trade." *Globe and Mail* 13 Apr. 1985, "Books": 7.

——. "Alice Drops Her Cigarette on the Floor. . . ." *Canadian Literature* 91 (1981): 10–21.

——. "Bragg and Minna." *Stones*. Markham, ON: Viking, 1988. 3–26.

——. *The Butterfly Plague*. New York: Viking, 1969.

——. *The Butterfly Plague*. Rev. ed. Markham, ON: Penguin, 1986.

——. *Can You See Me Yet?* Ed. Peter Hay. Introd. Margaret Laurence. Talonplays. Vancouver: Talonbooks, 1977.

——. "A Chat with Timothy Findley." With Julie Hobson. *Stage Write* [London, ON] Mar.–May 1993: 1–2.

——. "Christmas Remembered." *Chatelaine* Dec. 1979: 43+.

——. *Dinner Along the Amazon*. Penguin Short Fiction. Markham, ON: Penguin, 1984.

——. *Famous Last Words*. Toronto: Clarke, 1981.

——. "The Gould Standard." *Saturday Night* Apr. 1989: 71–72.

——. *Headhunter: A Novel*. Toronto: HarperCollins, 1993.

——. "In Memoriam: A Trial and a Joy." *Books in Canada* Apr. 1985: 18–19.

——. "Inquest." *Books in Canada* Mar. 1989: 11–13.

——. *Inside Memory: Pages from a Writer's Workbook*. Toronto: HarperCollins, 1990.

———. Interview. With Warren Davis. *The Day It Is.* CBC Television, Toronto. 27 Oct. 1967.

———. "Interview with Timothy Findley." With Alison Summers. *Canadian Literature* 91 (1981): 49–55.

———. *John A. — Himself!* Dir. Peter Moss. Theatre London, London, ON. 31 Jan.–17 Feb. 1979.

———. "The Journey: A Montage for Radio." *Canadian Drama/ L'Art dramatique canadien* 10.1 (1984): 115–40.

———. *The Last of the Crazy People.* New York: Meredith, 1967.

———. "Lemonade." *Dinner Along the Amazon.* Penguin Short Fiction. Markham, ON: Penguin, 1984. 1–64.

———. "Long Live the Dead: An Interview with Timothy Findley." With Johan Aitken. *Journal of Canadian Fiction* 33 (1981–82): 79–93.

———. *Matinee.* CBC Radio, Toronto, 6 Jan. 1971.

———. "My Final Hour: An Address to the Philosophy Society, Trent University, Monday, 26 January 1987." *Journal of Canadian Studies/Revue d'études canadiennes* 22.1 (1987): 5–16.

———. "The Mystery of Violence." With Suzanne Sandor. *Maclean's* 27 Oct. 1986: 10–12.

———. "The Name's the Same." *Stones.* Markham, ON: Viking, 1988. 133–47.

———. *Not Wanted on the Voyage.* Markham, ON: Penguin, 1985.

———. "Otto-Eroticism." *This Magazine* Oct.–Nov. 1990: 18.

———. "The People on the Shore." *Dinner Along the Amazon.* Penguin Short Fiction. Markham, ON: Penguin, 1984. 133–48.

———. Personal Interview. 12 Aug. 1992.

———. "Prize-Winning Author Did Manual Labor: My First Job." With Gord Gates. *Toronto Star* 27 July 1982: A2.

———. "The Return of the Crazy People." With Peter Buitenhuis. *Books in Canada* Dec. 1988: 17–20.

———. *The Stillborn Lover.* Winnipeg: Blizzard, 1993.

———. *Stones.* Markham, ON: Viking, 1988.

———. "Stratters, Ont." *Festival Stratford: 1988 Visitors' Guide.* Stratford, ON: Stratford Festival and Stratford and Area Visitors' and Convention Bureau, 1988. 4.

———. "The Tea Party, or How I Was Nailed by Marian Engel, General Booth and Minn Williams Burge." *Room of One's Own* 9.2 (1984): 35–40.

———. *The Telling of Lies: A Mystery.* Markham, ON: Viking, 1986.

———. "Timothy Findley." With Alan Twigg. *Strong Voices: Conversations with Fifty Canadian Authors.* Ed. Alan Twigg. Madeira Park, BC: Harbour, 1988. 83–89.

———. "Timothy Findley." With Alberto Manguel. *Descant* 16.4–17.1 (1985–86): 229–38.

———. "Timothy Findley." With Graeme Gibson. *Eleven Canadian Novelists.* Ed. Graeme Gibson. Toronto: Anansi, 1973. 115–49.

———. "Timothy Findley." With Terry Goldie. *Kunapipi* [Aarhus, Den.] 6.1 (1984): 56–67.

———. "Timothy Findley: Make Peace with Nature, Now." With Donald Cameron. *Conversations with Canadian Novelists.* Ed. Donald Cameron. Toronto: Macmillan, 1973. 49–63.

———. "True Tales of Toronto: The King and Mrs. Simpson." *Toronto Life* May 1984: 32–33.

———. "An Unforgettable Journey to Russia." *Bad Trips.* Ed. Keath Fraser. New York: Vintage, 1991. 48–58.

———. "War." *Dinner Along the Amazon.* Penguin Short Fiction. Markham, ON: Penguin, 1984. 65–81.

———. *The Wars.* Toronto: Clarke, 1977.

———. "Writer Timothy Findley." With Patricia Black. *Scene* [London, ON] 25 Mar.–7 Apr. 1993: 3.

Fitzgerald, Judith. "From The Wars to a Blind Cat on the Ark." *Globe and Mail* 2 July 1983, "Entertainment": 3.

Fulford, Robert. "Deep in the South (of Ontario)." Rev. of *The Last of the Crazy People,* by Timothy Findley. *Toronto Star* 29 July 1967: 26.

Galloway, Myron. "Findley's Wars." Rev. of *The Wars,* by Timothy Findley. *Montreal Star* 6 May 1978: D3.

Gardner, David. "Eros and Thanatos." *ArtsCanada* Apr. 1968: 25–26.

Gefen, Pearl Sheffy. "Scenes and Variations." *Globe and Mail* 5 July 1991: C1+.

Godfrey, Stephen. "Noah's Ark Sets Sail on Stage." *Globe and Mail* 28 Mar. 1991: C3.

Good, Cynthia. "Timothy Findley: Author of the Year." *Canadian Bookseller* June–July 1984: 12.

Graham, June. "The Children of Dionysus." CBC *Times* 24–30 July 1965: 10–11.

Henry, Martha. Letter to the author. 24 Mar. 1992.

Hill, Douglas. "Powerful, Devastating Canadian War Novel Demands Superlatives." Rev. of *The Wars*, by Timothy Findley. *Toronto Star* 22 Oct. 1977: D7.

Huftel, Sheila. *Arthur Miller: The Burning Glass*. New York: Citadel, 1965.

Hulcoop, John F. "Timothy Findley." *Canadian Writers Since 1960*. First Series. Ed. W.H. New. Detroit: Gale, 1986. 181–91. Vol. 53 of *Dictionary of Literary Biography*. 130 vols. to date. 1978– .

Hutt, William. Personal interview. 26 Aug. 1992.

Kirchhoff, H.J. "*The Stillborn Lover* a Grand Coup." Rev. of *The Stillborn Lover*, by Timothy Findley. Grand Theatre, London, ON. *Globe and Mail* 29 Mar. 1993: C3.

Lacey, Liam. " 'See-Worthy' But Not Ship-Shape." Rev. of *Not Wanted on the Voyage*, adapt. by Richard Rose and D.D. Kugler. Based on Timothy Findley's *Not Wanted on the Voyage*. Canadian Stage, Toronto. *Globe and Mail* 15 Feb. 1992: C4.

Laurence, Margaret. Introduction. *Can You See Me Yet?* By Timothy Findley. Ed. Peter Hay. Talonplays. Vancouver: Talonbooks, 1977. 9–13.

Lehmann-Haupt, Christopher. "Books of the Times." Rev. of *Famous Last Words*, by Timothy Findley. *New York Times* 22 June 1982: C10.

McCloskey, Dennis. "For the Love of Writing." *Canadian Living* May 1991: 73–76.

MacFarlane, David. "The Perfect Gesture." *Books in Canada* Mar. 1982: 5–8.

Manguel, Alberto. "Findley's People." Rev. of *Dinner Along the Amazon*, by Timothy Findley. *Books in Canada* June–July 1984: 13+.

Marchand, Philip. "Findley Takes on Shrinks." *Toronto Star* 18 Apr. 1993: C3.

———. "Timothy Findley: Novelist on a High Wire." *Chatelaine* Feb. 1983: 44+.

Martin, Peter. "An Alternate Selection." Rev. of *The Wars*, by Timothy Findley. *Canadian Reader* Oct. 1977: 6–7.

Moreira, Peter. "Mystery Findley's Obvious Genre." Rev. of *The Telling of Lies*, by Timothy Findley. *Chronicle-Herald* [Halifax] 8 Nov. 1986: 27.

Moss, John. "Timothy Findley." *A Reader's Guide to the Canadian Novel*. 2nd ed. Toronto: McClelland, 1987. 108–18.

Novak, Barbara. "Brilliant Short Stories All Touch on Madness." Rev. of *Stones*, by Timothy Findley. *London Free Press* 10 Dec. 1988: D12.

Park, Darcie. "Findley Finds Play Stunning." *Winnipeg Free Press* 11 Jan. 1992: C27.

Parton, Margaret. "A Sad Song of Eleven Summers." Rev. of *The Last of the Crazy People*, by Timothy Findley. *Saturday Review* 5 Aug. 1967: 36–37.

Pearce, John. Personal interview. 27 Aug. 1992.

Percy, H.R. "Along Findley's Amazon a Jungle of Despair." Rev. of *Dinner Along the Amazon*, by Timothy Findley. *Quill & Quire* Aug. 1984: 30.

Roberts, Paul. "Findley's Name-Dropping Epic a Major Triumph." Rev. of *Famous Last Words*, by Timothy Findley. *Quill & Quire* Nov. 1981: 23.

Ross, Val. "High Colour, Deep Shadow." *Globe and Mail* 15 May 1993: C1+.

Schiefer, Nancy A. "Fascist High Times Brilliantly Portrayed." Rev. of *Famous Last Words*, by Timothy Findley. *London Free Press* 28 Nov. 1981: B11.

Stedmond, J.M. "Letters in Canada: 1967. Fiction." Rev. of *The Last of the Crazy People*, by Timothy Findley. *University of Toronto Quarterly* 37 (1968): 386.

*Timothy Findley: Anatomy of a Writer*. Videocassette. Dir. Terence Macartney-Filgate. National Film Board, 1992. 57 min., 25 sec.

Wesley, Dave. "NFB Catches Findley at His Most Generous." *Spectator* [Hamilton] 18 Jan. 1992: C2.

Whitehead, William. Personal interview. 13 Aug. 1992.

Whittaker, Herbert. "Flamboyant Personality an Aid to Russian Actor." *Globe and Mail* 7 Dec. 1955: 7.

Woodcock, George. "History to the Defeated: Some Fictions of Timothy Findley." *Northern Spring: The Flowering of Canadian Literature*. Vancouver: Douglas, 1987. 159–77.

York, Lorraine. "Songs and Whispers." *Brick* 40 (1991): 60–62.

PRINTED IN CANADA